Sports Writing

Books in the 'Writing Handbooks' series

Freelance Writing for Newspapers • Jill Dick

The Writer's Rights • Michael Legat

Writing for Children • Margaret Clark

Writing Crime Fiction • H.R.F. Keating

Writing Erotic Fiction • Derek Parker

Writing about Food • Jenny Linford

Writing Fantasy Fiction • Sarah LeFanu

Writing Historical Fiction • Rhona Martin

Writing Horror Fiction • Guy N. Smith

Writing for Magazines • Jill Dick

Writing a Play • Steve Gooch

Writing Popular Fiction • Rona Randall

Writing for Radio • Rosemary Horstmann

Writing for the Teenage Market • Ann de Gale

Writing for Television • Gerald Kelsey

Writing a Thriller • André Jute

Writing about Travel • Morag Campbell

Other books for writers

Writers' and Artists' Yearbook

Word Power: a guide to creative writing • Julian Birkett

Research for Writers • Ann Hoffmann

Interviewing Techniques for Writers and Researchers • Susan Dunne

Sports Writing

Alison Kervin

A&C Black • London

First published 1997
A&C Black (Publishers) Limited
35 Bedford Row, London WC1R 4JH

ISBN 0–7136–4648–9

A CIP catalogue record for this book
is available from the British Library.

Photograph by Graham Chadwick, reproduced by permission of ALLSPORT

Typeset in 10/11.7 pt Palatino
Printed and bound in Great Britain by Redwood Books, Trowbridge, Wilts

CONTENTS

INTRODUCTION

Although the idea of travelling around the world to cover your favourite sport, meeting stars and occasionally writing incisive articles, is very appealing, the reality of high-level sports journalism is that it's a deadline-filled, nit-picking and lonely profession in which your whole life has to be dedicated to sport. It can be great fun, but most of the time there has to be such an attention to detail that you spend as much time worrying about exactly who the replacement scrum-half used to play for than you spend extolling the virtues of a timely drop goal!

Sports journalism is a specialism. It is taken seriously by newspapers and magazines because it sells. You have to be utterly professional to cover it properly, because there is nothing in the world that's more 'newsy' and up-to-the-minute than a sports event. If you're an athletics correspondent covering a race, you have to know as the first runner hits the tape whether his time is better or worse than the last time he ran, whether it's good enough, whether there are any surprise finishing positions and how the results compare with the results from Zurich the week before. At the back of your mind you need to have a list of key questions to ask him at the interview after the event, when you'll have about 15 other journalists to fight through for a 20-second quote. Throughout most rugby and football matches, there will be sports writers constantly on the phone, filing their stories at 15-minute intervals. They then have 15 minutes after the final whistle to file an introduction to go on the top of the piece, before rushing to the press conference to get some quotes for the second edition.

The best sports journalists are extremely knowledgeable, have brilliant contacts and an over-riding passion for the sport that they are covering. They will tend to be cynical, but deep down they believe in what they are covering – they have to, in order to do it any justice at all. Their job can sometimes be wonderful and brilliantly fulfilling; it is always taxing; and – like in most areas of journalism – the low points can be dreadful.

Whether you're interested in winning the Sports Journalist of the Year award, or just in putting together a match report about your local team that will get into the local paper, there are the same key rules to follow and the same advice that is relevant. If you approach the subject rationally and are determined enough, getting yourself on the sports journalism ladder in some way is not too difficult. Because of the profusion of publications which now touch upon sport in some way, there should be some avenue that you can explore to get yourself published.

This book looks at how you can get started, where you go from there, and how you can reach your goals in the simplest but most effective way possible.

1 • HOW TO START

The life of a sports journalist is one full of colour, excitement and constant challenge. The variety is immense – from the very grand and glamorous one day, to the downright dull and uninteresting the next.

Unfortunately for would-be sports journalists, it is the glitz and glamour that attracts all the attention, so thousands of people hanker after jobs as sports journalists. This can make the task of getting work in sports journalism (and ultimately making the transition from interested and knowledgeable fan to inspired and respected sports writer) extremely difficult.

Most frustrating of all, there are plenty of people around who are happy to work for nothing, just to get their name in print or to get a break in the profession. In the low-budget world of local newspapers, these people will often be doing the work. Since local newspapers are the stepping stones to top journalism jobs, it can be very annoying when you are trying to get started and need to make some money from the profession. Added to this is the fact that jobs come up very rarely. You will often find that the same person has been doing the local hockey reports for the past 10 years and that he has become something of a local institution, making it difficult for anyone else to 'muscle' their way in.

However, don't despair completely. Every year, hundreds of new journalists join the profession. The media generally is expanding all the time, making room for far more writers and broadcasters. So how do you succeed? Obviously luck and good timing can play a part. If you happen to send a letter off to an editor just as the newspaper is looking for a freelance football writer, you may find it the easiest move in the world to start your career. But luck and good timing are in the hands of the gods – what is in your hands is the opportunity to make sure that you have done all you can to prepare yourself properly before you set out. This is where this book will help you. There are not too many short cuts if you want to maximise your chances of success, and much of it depends on hard work.

If you are already a journalist or writing a great deal in your current profession, then much of this chapter will contain information you are already familiar with. If, however, you are starting from scratch with no experience in the profession, it's worth reading through to give yourself an idea of what will be expected from you, and the different ways in which you can acquire the necessary skills to get started.

If you think you already have these skills, chapter two will outline how you move on, and plan your campaign. Chapter three shows you how to contact an editor. Chapters four and five look at the profession in more depth, then the rest of the book is devoted to looking at the market place, and at what areas of the media are available to the sports journalist.

Starting at the beginning

If you have never written a word before, but have always wanted to be a sports writer, start by thinking through what the key characteristics of a sports writer are. Think too about what qualities you will need to acquire and display in order to succeed.

There are lots of criteria for judging whether a sports journalist is good or bad – no two journalists are the same, they all have very different attributes (indeed, it is often individual flair that marks a journalist out). But the following characteristics are common among all sports writers, whether freelance or full-time, and whatever area of the industry they are working in. These skills are best remembered by the acronym: WUCKNUPA, which stands for:

- Writing skills
- Understanding your publication and the market that it exists in
- Contacts
- Knowledge of your chosen sport
- Nose for a good story
- Uniqueness – do you stand out from the crowd?
- Passion for the sport
- Accuracy, fairness, responsibility and reliability

Having read through all these attributes, you need to decide whether or not you think you have any of them before you start. Or do you at least have the ability to acquire them? If you work to try and understand all of these areas you will have a much better chance of being able to answer an editor's complicated questions at interview; you will also have the skills to succeed when you get a job. The wider your vocabulary of skills, and the more holistic your approach to sports journalism in the early stages, the better your chances of getting involved.

Obviously, journalists divide according to which of the above skills they specialise in. Someone who really understands the market-place, writes well and has an enormous passion for the sport may well end up with a senior job on a specialist publication; whereas those writers who have great contacts and can always spot the angle might write for tabloid papers. If your writing skills are not great but you have a passion for a sport and great contacts, you might end up as a researcher on a specialist sports television programme.

We will take the above skills one at a time and look at them in more depth:

Can you write?

This seems like an obvious question to ask someone who wants to be a sports journalist. Of course you think you can write, or you wouldn't be reading this book; but have you ever tried writing a match report or doing an interview with restrictions on time and space? You may have been able to reel off wonderful essays when you had a month to write them, but what if you've only got an hour? And what if your piece is for hundreds of thousands of readers and not just one teacher?

Being able to write is the most obvious asset for a sports journalist, or indeed any journalist – but it's amazing how many people think they can become sports journalists simply because they enjoy sport and read a lot about it.

You don't have to be Shakespeare to write match reports, but you do have to be able to write coherently and logically. The first step is simple: have a go at writing something and see whether you can do it. An easy way to start is to choose a local sporting event. It can be anything at all, but it's vital that you watch the whole event and that the local paper also covers it (if you go regularly to a particular match or event, you will know whether the press is usually there – you could even call the club and ask them if the press will be there, or just call the paper themselves). Then watch the event with a pen and paper and make notes throughout. Write up a report afterwards (*see* chapter five for help in structuring a match report). You can then see exactly how your report compares to the one that appears in the papers. Obviously, if the paper you are monitoring yourself against is the one you are keen to write for eventually, this is the best test of all.

Try to write within set time-scales like the journalists on the paper do. If you give yourself hours and hours to put it together, it won't be realistic. Chances are that if it's a Saturday match, the journalists will have to file their reports first thing on Monday morning. It's therefore important that you don't leave the writing too long – put it together when you're as fresh as possible, and can remember clearly what happened.

This book will give you lots of ideas about making it in sports journalism, and lots of tips for putting sports stories together, but it can't actually teach you how to write, or how to put the effort and thought into writing a piece – that has to come from you. Writing can be an intensely personal occupation, and it can be difficult to be honest with yourself and unbiased about what you've achieved. At the end of the day, however, you have to look at what you've written and make an honest judgement. Try to work out where you've gone wrong and how you can improve. Are all the facts right? Are all the names spelt properly? Have you told the story accurately? Is the report interesting? It's much easier to read someone else's match report and think you can do better than it is to write the thing from scratch yourself; so have a go at writing a report from the beginning, and see how you cope.

If you can't think of a local event that would be suitable for you to experiment on, but would quite like to have a go at writing up a match report, then you could try reporting on a live event on television. Make sure you turn the sound down so that you're not influenced by the commentators' views and opinions. Take notes throughout the match, then write up a 500-word match report afterwards and compare what you have written with what appears in the papers the next day. It may help to give you an idea of what your writing skills are like, and how you cope under the pressure of writing a stated number of words by a given time. Many local newspapers coach their new reporters by sending them to events with a trained reporter, getting them to write up a story afterwards which they then compare with that of the experienced reporter. It can be a scary feeling for the new journalist, and it feels very much like 'sink or swim'; but it does give you an instant impression of how near the mark you are.

If you're full of confidence about your writing ability, you could go along to a local football match and watch, then write up a report. If you submit it to a local paper and request any comments, you may find some kindly soul who remembers what it was like when they first started and who is willing to help you by giving you key pointers. Don't send the report for the personal attention of the editor, because he won't have time to help. Instead, write in requesting information and help from any journalist on the sports desk.

The only way of knowing whether you're on the right track is to read other journalists' reports and analyse your own work as carefully and dispassionately as possible. The other way of knowing whether you're on the right track is to research carefully.

Understanding the publication and its market

There is a big difference between preparing an article for the editor of *The Telegraph* and writing a piece for the editor of a local paper. The latter requires a strong local angle and information that is relevant to local residents; whereas the former has to interest people all over Britain, so it has to focus on much wider, national issues.

You need to understand the specific demands of the publication you want to write for, and exactly what they want from their journalists. Can you expect your introductory letter and ideas to be appropriate if you don't even know who the magazine is targeting itself at? Of course not – you need to have a clear idea of who the magazine's targeting before you can effectively target the magazine.

In addition to understanding who the publication is targeting, you also need to understand the complexities of the market-place in which it is operating. For example, who is its keenest competitor and how does it compare to its rivals? Is it the market leader? How is it positioned in the market? It's useful to think of these things in terms of style, design, price and content. Look at things like the cover of a magazine or the front page of a newspaper. The advertisements will also give you an idea of where the newspaper is pitching itself. What promotions do they run? What pictures – are they all stock photos, or is every photo shoot specially commissioned? Do they do any branding or merchandising? Try to get an impression about the whole package and who they are gearing themselves to.

The most common cry from editors as they receive feature ideas is, "Don't they read the publication? We'd never run something like that," or "We did that two weeks ago". The very least an editor expects is that you will know about the publication that you are aspiring to write for. You will instantly alienate an editor if you write to him suggesting an interview with a player if it turns out that the player is a columnist for the magazine, and has been involved with them for years!

So study the publication or publications you want to write for in great detail. You have to be sure to understand exactly who they target, what areas they cover and what their aims are.

Have you got good contacts?

Do you have a little black book brimming with telephone numbers? Or, at the very least, do you know whose numbers it would be useful to have, and how to get hold of them if you need to? Do you know who you should be cultivating a friendly working relationship with? You must be fairly involved in sport, or think you would like to be, to have bought this book in the first place; but do you know the people who make the decisions in your chosen sport? Could you call on them for quotes? Interviews? News and views? At any time?

Having contacts does not always mean having a direct line to Alan Shearer's house. It means knowing how easily you can get hold of the key people in your particular area when you need them. It may be the case that becoming friendly with the chairman of the local club is all you need, because he has so much influence that the players and the other club officials do what he says. Alternatively, you may have to make an effort to get to know every individual player from the youths to the vets, and regularly make time to renew your acquaintances. Having lots of contacts is obviously better than having one main contact – that person may leave!

Every time a new person joins the club, or a new manager, coach or official is appointed, you will have to make yourself known to them. Most journalists have a bulging contacts book, and know who all the key people to get to know are. No-one will expect you to arrive for an interview on a local paper with fantastic international sporting and media contacts, but if you want very quickly to become a correspondent for a particular sport, you will have to develop contacts rapidly. If your aim is to write for a bigger paper or specialist magazine, you will be expected to arrive with an impressive list of contacts. The only way to develop contacts is to keep going to sports events – and to keep talking to people.

You will have to be fairly pushy and go round introducing yourself, and asking questions and names (be sure to remember them!); but the more people you know, the more stories you'll get and the better journalist you'll eventually become. The usefulness of your contacts depends on them as individuals and what their attitude to the press is, as well as on what your relationship with them is like and how effectively you can 'court' them. Good contacts are invaluable – never underestimate them.

Knowledge of the sport

It's no good aspiring to be the world's leading golf correspondent if you don't really know much about the sport. Being able to play off an impressive handicap is all very admirable, but the reality of sports journalism is that at midnight in the office you have to be able to recognise the 14th-placed Scottish golfer by the back of his head for a picture caption.

Whether you're keen to become the greatest sports writer in the world, or just to write for the local paper, you need to understand the context of the sport you're writing about. How much of an expert are you? *Make* yourself an expert – it's vitally important. Have opinions, feel passionate. Know the characters, know the news stories, understand the politics, or you'll come unstuck.

It's not just basic information that you need at your disposal. Knowing who is the best squash player and which racquets you think are the best will not give you enough knowledge to head up a squash magazine. Who are the best players and why are they the best? What are their major achievements; why are these achievements so important? As a journalist you will have to delve far deeper into the sport than knowing about an individual race or event. You will need to know the 'ins and outs' of a player's route to the event: for example, when did they win certain matches? What were the scores? Ask yourself too how the sport is developing and who makes the decisions.

Do you think you're an authority on your chosen sport? You really need to be able to impress with your understanding of it if you want to be taken seriously.

It's not just the top sportsmen and women that you have to know about. Discover the ones coming up the ranks – the players of the future. For instance, you may know what time Linford Christie completed his last eight races in, and what his World Record is, but do you know who finished further down the order and how he has been progressing since? If you write to a national newspaper and tell them you'd like to do a feature on Linford Christie, they're not going to take you seriously. It's something they've already thought about and done a million times. Their athletics correspondent probably knows him personally and there's no way that they would use you to write an article rather than him. If, however, you research carefully and discover that there's a youngster coming up through the ranks who is emulating Linford Christie's times, you may be able to sell a feature on him to an athletics magazine or to a local newspaper. However, remember that it's likely the paper will have covered your story already unless it's a really radically new idea; specialist titles in particular tend to cover stories from all angles.

Thinking of ideas for stories can be one of the most difficult parts of being a freelance journalist, but if you really understand your sport and are enthusiastic and eager to find out more, you will find that there are dozens of unexplored avenues. Talk to people, read all you can and watch all you can. Keep your eyes and ears peeled at all times. I got a piece into *The Times* about the England rugby doctor after I discovered that he was practising in the area I had moved to, and I decided to register with him. Over a period of time I managed to get him to talk about life behind the scenes with the team. If I had not known his name, I would never have got the story. Do you know the names of all the ancillary staff in your sport?

Have you a nose for a good story?

Will a newspaper be able to rely upon you to come back with all the information if a story breaks when you're at a match? If your club's longest-serving player gets sent off for abusing fans, will you spot that it is an interesting angle for your local paper? Are you prepared to fight through other journalists to get an interview with him after the game?

In addition to being able to write coherently – and, most importantly, to a set brief and a set number of words by a set time – you also have to know enough about the sport to be able to come up with plenty of ideas all the time that no-one else has thought of. You won't always be contacted by the paper and commissioned to do things. Sports journalism can be as tough as any journalism, despite the perception that the political and 'hard news' journalists are taken seriously on newspapers, whereas the sports pages are written by enthusiasts in clubs. This is simply not true any more. The sports journalists are as passionate, enthusiastic and committed to writing about sport, uncovering the truths about sport and exposing malpractice in sport as the current affairs reporters are.

There are always contemporary politics which affect sports, and sports issues tend to reflect the general issues of the time. For example, while the South African apartheid problem was being examined on the front pages, there was a very real overlap into sport. As sporting teams refused to tour there, and players who went over there were black-listed from competing for Britain, sport found itself dragged into the major political debate of the day.

It is difficult to analyse your own ability to assess what is the main angle in a story. Certainly, anything in the national news that finds itself reflected in sport is automatically a 'good angle' for your story; but in every match, interview, feature or news item there will also be an individual 'angle' which you will have to learn to spot. If you miss an obvious 'hook' for an article, this could result in the whole piece looking flat and untimely so that it may not make it into the paper. If you have never written for a news publication before, the best way to work on looking for angles is described earlier in this chapter in relation to writing skills. Have a go and compare your results with those of a professional. Watch a match and decide what you think was the most important factor in that match. Then have a look at a printed match report, and see whether the professional journalists agree with your decision.

Chapter five looks at how you put a sports piece together and so might help to head you in the right direction. However, being able to spot what is the most important angle can depend as much on your knowledge of the sport and its participants as on your news sense. It might be worth emphasising this if the subject of your lack of news experience ever comes up at an interview – for example, if an editor asks you at interview whether you think your lack of news training will make it harder for you if a story breaks when you are out covering a match or event (i.e., crowd violence or drugs).

You should be aware that many newspapers are happier employing journalists who have been on a news training course of some description rather than journalists who come into the profession totally 'cold'. They think that the former will at least have some knowledge and experience of what is 'newsy', especially since journalism courses often ask you to spot the 'angle' in a given series of scenarios. What is considered 'newsy' depends as much on the publication you're writing for as the story itself. Like most things in journalism, the bottom line is common-sense, but you do also need to understand the sport to spot opportunities. For example, if you go to a rugby match and see the man with the No. 1 shirt on his back kicking, you may not be particularly interested if you don't know very much about rugby. If you understand the sport, though, you'll realise that No. 1 is a prop and one of the most unlikely candidates for a kicker. The fact that the prop was kicking would definitely be worth investigating with the club afterwards – ask them if he always kicks; if not, where's the usual kicker?

The more knowledge you have and the more research you do, the more unique angles you'll spot immediately. For example, a few phone calls after a match in which someone called Liam Botham was playing informed a key journalist that Liam was indeed a relation of Ian Botham – a nice angle, and one which others did not pick up on. Liam went on to become a good rugby player, but in the early days a quick-witted reporter got a good story which made all the nationals in addition to television and radio news.

What's your USP?

In business it's known as a USP – a Unique Selling Proposition. It describes what it is about a business's product that makes it unique in the market. As you try to sell yourself to an editor, you too should have a USP. What makes you stand out from the crowd? Why should anyone employ you when there are so many aspiring writers around?

In journalism, you may find yourself being asked to sell yourself more than you would in most job interviews. This is because you will not just be having a 'loose connection' with the product which your employers are selling – in journalism, unlike in most industries, you *are* that product. You're not going to be tucked away in some back room with no public contact; you are vitally important, because your words will make up the product and will therefore help to decide whether the product sells, whether advertisers are interested, and whether the company makes money or folds!

You create the whole purpose of the magazine's or newspaper's existence; therefore they have to make sure you're right and worth using. It's about more than the money they're paying you – it's about the publication's whole prestige. They're not going to let you loose on their readers if they can't trust you – and like every other industry in the world they haven't got time to waste – so they want to make sure that you know what you're doing, and they want to be able to let you get on with it without them having to check everything you write.

In order to convince people that you are unique and worth investing in, you have to have the WUCKNUPA characteristics in abundance. Ideally, too, you should have a specific area in which you feel you are unique or at least have enormous experience. Perhaps you're a former top-class player, or a coach at a leading club; or perhaps you can also take photographs, do cartoons, or sketch. Make sure you promote this as much as you can. Anything you can utilise to sound 'different' will help – your experience, the fact that you know everyone at the local club or used to serve on a committee, the fact that you once wrote a novel – anything at all. Then, when you talk to editors, it gives you something positive with which to sell yourself and it gives you a promotional tool when you come to write your letter. The newspaper or magazine may use your uniqueness when they come to use your work, for example: 'by former international hockey player, Jane Sixsmith'. They get reflected credibility, and you get work. Find yourself a USP – it definitely helps!

Do you have a real passion for the sport?

Playing a sport and enjoying it socially is very different from committing your working life to it. If you work full time on a particular sport it can soon lose its charm, especially if every phone call, every conversation and every picture you see, and every word you read or say revolves around it.

Does *every* area of the sport – from new coaching and fitness techniques to the latest wrangles over club finances and fixture clashes – excite you? Are you interested enough to watch everything you can about a sport? And talk to everyone you come across? You really will find yourself living and breathing sport if you pursue your ambition to become a sports journalist.

Every journalist will tell you that they're never off duty. If a local news journalist drives past an accident he'll always pull over to find out what's going on. He'll look for an eyewitness or get an exclusive 'on-the-spot' report. What is different about sports journalism is that the vast majority of the bread-and-butter, day-to-day stuff takes place in anti-social hours. You will find yourself working evenings and weekends as a matter of course; and that's before you start chasing any specific stories. The hours in sport can be extremely long because whilst the base of your work takes place during evenings and weekends, the mechanics of putting together a publication take place between 9.00 a.m. and 5.00 p.m.

Getting hold of people for quotes and interviews, particularly if you've only got work numbers for them, also takes place during the day. If you're not completely obsessed with your sport, and willing to pour every waking hour into writing and researching, thinking and talking about it, you will find yourself getting very resentful of the enormous amount of commitment that's required.

Accuracy

Getting a 'scoop' once in a while is wonderful, but *accuracy* is the cornerstone of good journalism, and it is absolutely vital that you learn to check, double check and triple check everything.

You can't afford to get peoples' names wrong or use inaccurate statistics. If you're not a perfectionist you may find it difficult to remember the importance of it, but the first time you make a mistake and the letters flood into the newspaper you'll learn a valuable lesson about how carefully sports fans read their publications!

It's not only statistics and names that have to be checked every time you interview someone. If anyone gives you information, you always have to check it because **even though it's not your mistake, if your name's on the piece it's always your responsibility.**

In sport, since much of the information is accrued through phone calls – collating results, getting team news, etc. – you need to make sure that every name you take over the phone is spelt out, and you need to double check any odd-sounding names with a separate source (the club, or ideally the person themselves). Anyone who's been mis-quoted, had their name mis-spelt or been referred to erroneously will know how frustrating it can be. Since in local sport you come across the same people week after week, you can't afford to upset anyone, let alone run the risk of legal action.

2 • PLANNING AND GOAL-SETTING

The planning stage

If you have done all the ground-work, and you think you have both the abilities outlined in chapter one and the confidence and enthusiasm to use them effectively in your work, what editor wouldn't take a chance with you? The answer's very simple – the editor who won't take a chance is the editor who doesn't believe you. It's not that anyone is going to think you are lying or trying to deceive them; it's just that anyone can write off to a magazine or newspaper and sell themselves as the greatest sports journalist ever to exist. What they *can't* do is prove to a busy editor that they are the right person for the job.

Proving yourself is paramount to your success. If you went to a job interview and told the interviewer that you were a brilliant artist, the very least he would expect is that you have a couple of paintings with you to prove it. Similarly, you can't walk into an editor's office and proclaim that you are a brilliant writer if you haven't written anything before.

As you come to the planning stage, and start setting goals for yourself, you must be properly prepared. Whilst working to achieve the goals that you have set yourself, make sure you keep this fact in the back of your mind: you need to be able to prove to an editor that you have the necessary skills.

Plan of action

The best way to start is to draw up a plan of action. Abstractly writing off to every newspaper and magazine without thinking through what you're doing will only lead to disappointment, and it may put you off for ever if your first attempt comes flying back to you with a rejection slip as quickly as you sent it.

It's worth spending some time trying to work out exactly what it is that you want to achieve. It helps if you can get into the habit of writing everything down, remaining completely clear about what your aims are and how you are going to achieve them before you start.

People will tell you that publishing is full of knock-backs and that you have to be fairly thick-skinned to survive. You will definitely be able to eliminate at least some of those knock-backs if you are properly prepared. Even if your aim is just to write a short piece for the local newspaper, it helps if you can be as business-like about it as possible and prepare everything well.

However, if there's just one local paper in your area, and if you only know about one sport, what happens when that local paper writes back and says it's not interested? Is that the end of all your hopes of becoming a sports writer, or have you got a back-up plan? If your dream is to become a sports writer, then *goals* are your way of translating that dream into a series of small achievable steps. A plan of action describes what those steps will encompass.

Why is goal-setting important?

Goal-setting may sound like a rather pompous business term to be using in a book about sports writing, but it is the way in which all our top sportspeople work on mapping out their objectives and targets. It is a great way of making sure that you really know where you want to be, and of establishing – before you start on a project – exactly what you have to do to get there. It also focuses you on what you are trying to achieve, in the same way that athletes use goal-setting to set targets, define aims and measure achievements.

Setting goals allows you to monitor and motivate yourself, and shows you a pathway to where you want to be. There may be a few hurdles to leap along the way (for example, time, equipment, getting credibility, etc.), but if you consider these at the beginning and don't think you can jump over them, you can work towards ways in which you can run around them! For example, you may have bought this book because you are a sports fan who was good at English when at school or university. Your day job may involve communication skills, so you feel fairly confident in your own writing ability. A couple of hurdles which immediately spring to mind are:

- Even though you think you're a good writer, you can't prove it to an editor. You haven't got a portfolio or a cuttings file to show, so why should anyone believe that you can do it?
- Do you understand the publication well enough to write off to the editor, or should you do more background research first? You will be one of dozens of people who write into editors every week. The magazine that I edit is the biggest-selling rugby magazine in the world, and after every Five Nations match we are inundated with match reports that people send in. In fact, we commission match reports for the Five Nations games around three months before the tournament kicks off, so all of the others get sent back. This is no reflection on the individual contributions.

Someone who doesn't think these things through carefully beforehand may find themselves extremely disappointed when they get rejected after putting in a great deal of work.

How to start goal-setting

The first thing to do is sit down and think realistically about what ultimately you would like to achieve. Are you looking for a career change? Do you want to dabble in writing for a local paper, or to become the best sports writer that ever existed?

Write down your ultimate goal at the bottom of a sheet of paper, and then write NOW at the top. You now have to work out a way of charting a route down the paper until you reach your ultimate goal. If you are 86 years old and your ultimate goal is to become the greatest sports writer that ever lived, you may find that the obstacles which you unearth on the way down the pathway end up being too obtrusive to allow you to achieve your goal! You will only find this out by thinking clearly and realistically about what your aims are, and what your experience, time and abilities will allow. For now, though, just write down what you really want – the realism can come later!

Once you have done this, work out what you have to do to achieve your goal. Make a list of *short-term*, *mid-term* and *long-term goals* on the route to achieving your objective.

Example

A 37-year-old PE teacher wants to change professions and become a full-time football reporter for a regional evening newspaper. He has some limited experience of writing because he occasionally sends in pieces about how the school side has been doing. Some of these have appeared in the local weekly paper.

His main objective is to become a regular football correspondent writing for the big regional evening paper. One of his short-term goals would be to put together a file of all the match reports he's had published so far, and concentrate on covering all school events for the local papers until he has an impressive file. He may even look to start up a school newsletter to convince future employers of his abilities.

Another short-term goal would be to contact the paper that he has been writing for and ask them for any advice. Since he has written for them before, making contact should not be too difficult, and he has the sporting credibility through his background in PE. He might also try to learn all he can about local football and turn himself into a recognised expert on the subject.

A mid-term goal would be to go along to local matches and cover them on a casual basis, and perhaps to write articles for the match-day programme. He could also start thinking of ideas for features and start writing them all down; he could research every area of the paper he's keen to work on so he understands how it pitches its match reports, and how this differs from what he's been doing on a local paper.

A long-term goal would be to send his cuttings file to the sports editor of the regional paper with ideas for features and a letter which impresses with his knowledge of local football. This is a long-term goal because if he writes off too soon – before doing the ground-work – he might ruin his chances completely. He then needs to follow up his letter with phone

calls and frequent communication with the sports editor, football correspondents and other sports staff until they are convinced of his commitment
and ability.

The *hurdles* which he may face along the way are as follows: his school
side may play on Saturdays, therefore he can't cover local Saturday
matches. He might have difficulty finding transport to matches; or have
too little time to get reports done for an evening paper and filed accurately
while trying to hold down a full-time job.

Obviously, if he is committed to becoming a football correspondent
and there isn't an opening locally, he may have to travel further afield to
find one. If he's done all the ground-work and sent the letter into the
regional paper with his cuttings file, the newspaper may turn him down
but know of openings with other papers in the area – or it might at least
be able to advise him.

He would eventually have to mail-shot a selection of regional papers
with his CV and sample cuttings, trying to convince them of his fund-
amental knowledge of the sport and emphasising how quickly he accrued
knowledge in his present locality.

Can you use the above example to think of some ways in which you can
start mapping out goals? The rest of this book will help you – but hopefully you will already have some ideas of your own.

If your goal is to write freelance, think about what the publication
currently covers, and what you could offer that's new and exciting. For
example, you may be interested in writing about some local badminton
matches and some interesting characters on the badminton scene that you
have come across in the course of your leisure time.

As a short-term goal, you would have to do your research and check
that no-one is covering the badminton club at the moment. If they are, you
may be able to get work alongside them; but if there's no-one doing it, you
have an angle with which to contact an editor. You also have a USP to
promote, because you are offering something unique – an insight into a
sport which they have not previously covered and the possibility of some
new readers.

Once you have established the situation regarding current coverage of
your chosen sport, you may try to come up with some ideas, or send in
samples of short news items and reports of tournaments being played
locally. Your long-term goal would be to cover all the local badminton
events. You may even re-think your plan if you are successful, and look to
start covering other minority sports or have a sports round-up column of
all those sports that don't currently get a mention.

Whatever you want to do, and whatever your goals turn out to be –
however ambitious or small they may appear when you start to analyse
them – write them down and start to think about what you need to do in
order to achieve them.

Once you've written down your ideal goals, it's time to read them through and to inject a little realism. You must decide whether they are all achievable. If they aren't, then maybe you need to set different goals to get yourself into a position where you can work up to the main objective. For example, if you've never written anything before, don't imagine that you will be able to waltz into the *Daily Telegraph* and get a commission to interview Andre Agassi. You have to start at the bottom and work your way up. There are some short cuts, especially if you've got a 'name' in a particular sport, or a particular knowledge or understanding – but you'll usually need to identify goals along your path to the top!

Finding the proof

Without any doubt, the area in which most would-be sports journalists fall down is in *proving* their skills to an editor. You can write all the letters in the world, and tell everyone that you can write well and would always be able to come up with a story, but you have to be able to prove it. There's an old adage in journalism: you're only as good as your last story. People don't care as much about where you went to school and what you do in your spare time as they do about seeing that you can write well. If you have a cuttings file brimming with proof that you can write in a number of styles, for a variety of newspapers and with some really interesting angles, it is only a matter of time before an editor will reply to you and commission work from you. If you have none of these, you must make it a primary goal to get as much proof together as possible. Only the very smallest of local newspapers will be happy to be treated as a training ground for up-and-coming reporters. Your favourite sports magazine or national newspaper will demand a certain amount of experience and some indication of talent and flair before they will take you seriously.

How do you prove yourself?

When you start to work out the plan of attack for achieving your goals, you'll soon discover that even though you've got certain skills, proving them to an editor who hasn't got the time to spare to take a chance with you can be extremely difficult. You need to have *tools* that you can produce which will show clearly and immediately that you know what you're doing. If we take the WUCKNUPA skills one by one (*see* chapter one), we can run through the various ways in which you can prove that you have the necessary competence.

1. Writing – the portfolio

The first thing you will have to do is prove to an editor – or whoever you write to – that you can write well. A well-written letter will show that you can string words together in a clean, accessible and readable fashion; but writing a letter that is targeted at one reader is very different from writing an article for a paper which has to inform and entertain thousands of readers. An editor will expect more proof of your writing skills than just a nicely typed letter. The best way to meet this burden of proof is to get a portfolio together. No matter what other goals you have, this should be a priority.

How do you get a portfolio together? What does it prove, and how do you go about showing it to an editor?

When you're first starting out, you may consider trying to write for match programmes, fanzines or even reporting on club newsines (phone-ins). Anything, really, which gives you experience of the news-gathering process and ultimately gets you a portfolio together.

If your company has its own magazine, you could set up a sports section to keep everyone up-to-date with what's doing on within company teams, locally or even nationally. If there is no company newsletter, why not try to start a sports bulletin.

Another idea might be to start really small, contacting papers, magazines or radio stations and offering to do voluntary work once a week. Even part-time helpers and those doing work experience can be given the chance to write something for publication if they are actually in the office when a story comes up. You may start off just taking the fishing reports over the phone, but if you're enthusiastic enough you will find that opportunities do come up, giving you the chance to write something which can start off a portfolio. You just need to get *something* into print to prove to an editor that you have got enough commitment and enough 'gumption' to get started in journalism. You won't be handed stories; you'll have to go out and get them. That's what the job is. So be prepared to create opportunities at the beginning in order to get a portfolio together.

2. Understanding the publication and the marketplace

As chapter one has emphasised, an editor will expect you to know enough about the newspaper or magazine to know what sort of reader it is trying to attract (i.e. its target audience) and what sort of features it runs. One reason that many aspiring writers are unsuccessful when they send off ideas is that those ideas are simply not appropriate for the publication. This is usually because the journalist sending them has done a blanket mail-shot without thinking of the particular demands of the magazine or newspaper. It may seem easy to put a list of ideas together and send it to every magazine or newspaper you can think of; but if you do that, you will only get a 'bite' by luck. If you happen to send the idea to a publication that runs stories like the one you're suggesting then you will be OK – otherwise, you'll receive little or no response for your efforts. And even if someone does call you to discuss your ideas, it will soon become apparent if they are not relevant or if they have not been thought through clearly enough.

So study the publication first, and prove that you understand it by mentioning in your letter some of the past articles that you have seen. You can also show that you understand the marketplace by mentioning rival titles and what they have been doing (obviously, outline why you think the publication you are writing to is better – but don't sound too desperate to work for them!).

3. Contacts

The best proof of your contact list is your portfolio! If you have had interviews with Mohammed Ali and Ben Johnson, no-one's going to argue with your sporting contacts. If, however, your contacts are limited to a few local people whom you have been getting to know since you started thinking about a career as a journalist, you have a slightly tougher battle on your hands.

The easiest way is to name-drop! When you come up with feature ideas, list the contacts you have at your disposal and to whom you would turn. For example, if you think that a series of features on the history of a local club would be interesting because it is 25 years since the club joined the league, you could list the contacts at the club who would be able to help you.

4. Knowledge of the sport

There are ways in which you can actually prove how knowledgeable you are about the technical side of sport. You can use tangible pieces of paper – certificates of coaching, refereeing, judging and training, for example – they can help to show commitment, dedication and knowledge about tactics on the pitch, on the track or in the pool. It may seem nothing to you if you did a preliminary swimming certificate at college, but at least it shows that you know the basics of the sport – which is more than you can prove without one!

But in sports journalism terms, there is much more to knowledge of a sport than understanding it in its most basic technical form. You will also have to convince an editor that you understand fully about the personalities behind the sport and the people in power – both in the sport generally, and in the sports club locally. This is essential, because understanding the dynamics of the sport will give you angles for news stories and leads for features and interviews. It is the holistic approach again – if you can try to satisfy every area of the skills that were listed in the first chapter, then you will really have the weapons at your disposal to fight off the questions that will come at you from all angles.

Understanding your sport in its broadest context rather than just understanding the tactics on the pitch is vital in your work as a journalist. For example, imagine if, suddenly, your local football club is told that it cannot move to the league above – despite winning promotion – because their ground isn't up to it. This is a big local story that may well make it into the nationals. You would want to talk to the officials at the club who are in charge of the ground, players who are frustrated at the situation – hopefully finding a player who thinks he will leave the club now because of all the problems – as well as to angry fans. At some stage you will need to get an official line on why the club's been turned down, so you need to know exactly who makes decisions like these. Are they made by the county organising body, the FA itself, or by some independent body?

You need to know a certain amount about the structure of the sport and the governing body to write up this and other such stories properly. You can prove to an editor that you know who is in charge and who makes key decisions by mentioning the key people you would contact for a story, and by emphasising that you understand what their role is and how they fit into the bigger pattern.

5. Nose for news

The ideas that you send into an editor need to reflect the fact that you have a good 'nose' for news and can spot an angle in a sports story. A newspaper needs to be sure that you are sharp enough to spot when something happens that would be of interest to their readers. This will, to a great extent, be reflected in the ideas you submit; so look for local angles on national stories so that the editor will see that you have been keeping up-to-date with what's in the news, and that you are able to spot when a national story can be given a local slant.

For example: crowd violence at a Brighton football match – what's the relevance of it in Leicester? Local angles might include:

- Talking to the Police about whether that sort of thing could ever happen in Leicester (i.e. 'Police are warning Leicester supporters that the sort of trouble that happened in Brighton could easily happen here.');
- Asking what is being done in Leicester to keep fans safe (talk to the club);
- Interviewing fans about whether they feel safe at matches;
- Researching the reasons for the trouble in Brighton, and asking if these are being eliminated in Leicester;
- Finding out if there is an expert in Leicester. At Leicester University there is a football hooliganism investigation bureau which co-ordinates all research in this area, so in this particular example there's a strong local angle that would work really well – even though it might not appear that way at the start.

Prove your nose for news by coming up with lots of different ideas all the time. If you get to meet an editor, talk to him or her about the hundreds of ideas that you've got, giving examples of good news stories that are being missed at the moment. For example, take the badminton instance discussed earlier in this section. Find out whether badminton is one of the most popular sports in the area, and how this compares with the national average. If you discover that badminton is one of the most popular sports in England, attracting 40% of all sports participants, but that in *your* area it is the most popular with a 60% following, then you could go to an editor with a strong news story – 20% more people than average play badminton regularly, and it is the most popular sport in Hastings. This would be a good story for the Hastings *Observer*, especially if they ran a tried and tested feature on the sport alongside the news story, produced a guide to local badminton clubs, and started doing regular club round-ups off the back of it. You might find yourself with a nice little side-line – but it all hinged on having the nose for that first news story and sending it off to an editor.

6. *Unique Selling Proposition*

When you write to an editor with a list of ideas, or send a CV, you are effectively trying to sell yourself. The first question the editor will ask is, 'Why should I buy this expertise? Why this person and not another?'

You need to prove to an editor that you are a good investment because you have something unique to offer. This can be anything from a history of playing sport in the area to a great contacts book or a brilliant nose for news – but you do need to try and shine in one particular area so that the editor remembers you when you leave the office.

If you have a history of playing, or any particular in-depth knowledge of the sport, do try and couch this in terms that can be easily remembered. For example, if you have been involved in the local club for 20 years don't just tell the editor that you have been involved for a long time – tell him or her that you have been going to the club for 20 years; that you've seen 13 chairmen come and go; that you've met 5000 different footballers and helped out on 2000 coaching nights; and that you have read over 400 programmes. Tell him or her that *this* is why you should be the club correspondent. It sounds much more unique and attractive than saying that you've been down at the club for quite a while and know most of the people there.

It's amazing how easy it is to come up with a couple of USPs once you start really thinking about it.

7. *Passion*

How do you prove that you are passionate about a sport? This is one of the most difficult things to prove, because you have to strike a careful balance. You must make sure that your enthusiasm for the subject matter is conveyed effectively, without seeming overawed and irrationally enthused by the whole thing. The newspaper wants fair and accurate reporting from a journalist – not a fan let loose on a typewriter!

The best way to prove you're passionate about the sport is by your commitment to it. If you have been going down to a local club for 20 years or more, and have seen players come and go, then it's definitely worth mentioning this long-term history of commitment because it's a USP and an indication of your passion for the sport.

However, you also need to make it clear that you understand the need for you to act entirely professionally. There is a temptation for people to think that sport is all about fun and leisure time. For many people it is. But not for you, if you want to make a career out of it. Even if you plan to put together sports reports in your spare time, you still need the discipline to watch a match or sporting event from an unbiased point of view, then you need to go home and write up the copy afterwards to a specific word count by a specific time (not as easy as it sounds!)

Many people who want to become sports journalists do so because they have been on club committees with the task of acting as press liaison officer, and they find they have a flair for this sort of work. It is important to remember the key differences between working as a press officer and working as a journalist. Most notably, as a press officer your job is to promote the work of the club; whereas as a journalist, your job is to give a fair and accurate report of the game. You can't sweep bad news under the carpet if you are going to be a good journalist. Despite what you have seen of some elements of the tabloid press, it's still true that the cornerstones of good journalism are accuracy and honesty. If the team plays abysmally, if someone is caught taking drugs or if there is any sort of financial scandal, you have to report those issues as enthusiastically as you report dynamic new signings or brilliant innings.

When considering a move into journalism, it is important to remember that the next time you go into the bar you may be treated very differently. Many sports journalists get on extremely well with the people they write about, but if you criticise someone's performance, you can be sure they will mention it next time you see them. So, whilst you can have very good friends in the profession, you have to remember that it's a business. There will be plenty of occasions on which you can socialise in the club bar and attend club functions, but it should be with the same level of commitment and detachment that you would carry out any business transaction.

8. *Accuracy*

Obviously, don't make spelling mistakes in your introductory letter! Or in any of the ideas you send in. Don't spell people's names incorrectly – check and double-check the spelling of the editor's name, and read through your letter until you are convinced that it is accurate.

I had an application for the post of deputy editor of *Rugby World* magazine, in which the candidate referred to *Rugby World* as *Rugby News* – our biggest rivals! The rest of the application was good, but it leaves you with a little doubt as to the person's real commitment. This is not because they made a slip, but because they didn't check the letter properly before sending it. Don't let something like this happen to you. Your letter is a chance for you to show that you can write coherently and logically, and it's a chance for you to sell your skills.

You should actually say in your letter, and certainly at interview, that you fully understand the importance of accuracy. Emphasise that you have a good nose for details and are punctilious in checking things. If you can prove this by citing examples, do so: for instance, 'I used to work in a shop where I had to check and double-check code numbers. I appreciate that it's different from reading and re-reading copy, but I assure you that in that job, I proved I had the concentration and patience to get it right.'

3 • MAKING CONTACT

First moves

Once you know which publication you want to work for, have your ideas organised and are confident that you have done enough background research to give you credibility and confidence, there are three ways in which you can proceed. You can either *phone* an editor, *turn up* at the door of an editor or *write* in to an editor.

Telephoning

It can be difficult to phone in, since you have no control over the way the conversation will proceed and you don't know how busy the editor will be when you talk to him. It also takes much more courage to phone up than it does to write a letter.

The editor might have three things happening at the same time, so that even if you come up with the best idea in the world, he is not going to stop, abandon everything and listen to you. He might also forget the conversation the minute he has put the phone down. On the positive side, it takes less time to phone than it does to draft a letter; you actually get to talk to the person making the decisions and will know instantly if he's interested; and – in the same way that it's harder for you to summon the courage to phone – it's harder for him to turn you down flat if you're on the phone to him. Sending a letter to say he's not interested in your piece is easy. If you think you've got a good feature idea and you want to get it over to the editor as quickly as possible, then phoning is a good idea if you've got the courage to do it.

Just turning up at the offices

This is never really a good idea. If you want to talk face to face with an editor, then it's much better to make an appointment with his secretary first. However, it is likely that they will suggest that you send in ideas and cuttings for him to look through first – so you may be back where you started anyway.

The only time to resort to turning up at the offices is if you've tried everything else, and you don't think you're getting through to the right person. In these circumstances, arriving with your cuttings in your hand and a list of ideas might do the trick.

However, don't do this if you're not properly prepared. If you've never written before, and you turn up and tell an editor that he should employ you immediately, he's bound to suggest that you go away and come back when you've got more experience.

Writing in

If you decide that sending in a letter is the best course of action, you have another choice to make: should you send in an article 'on spec', or should you send in a list of ideas for features which you think would be interesting and ask the editor to give you some feedback? Which of these you decide to do will probably depend more on how much work you have done on the piece than anything else – but the two options will be discussed in more detail later. Whichever course of action you decide to pursue, you will have to write a covering letter to accompany your submission. The letter you send in should be as professional as you can make it.

The letter

The basic advice is to keep your letter short, clear and to the point. There's really nothing to be gained from telling an editor all sorts of spurious details about your personal life or relating your entire life history, including when you went to school and what your parents do for a living. Make sure the editor can scan your letter quickly. If everything in the envelope is too wordy and will take too long to deal with, it is liable to sit in the editor's in-tray for a long time before anyone deals with it.

The following are worth remembering when you put together an initial letter. None of the points on their own will make or break your chances of working for the publication, but jointly they will help to create a more professional appearance, and this has got to help in terms of securing the work you want.

How should I address it?

The letter should always be addressed to someone specific. If you're not sure exactly who the right person is, make a big effort to find out. It is better to send it in to the wrong person in the team (i.e., if you send it to the deputy editor when all commissions are done by the features editor), than to send it in addressed to 'Dear Sir/Madam'. If you choose to address your letter to no-one specific, then you can guarantee that the wrong person will receive it and you'll be very lucky if anyone passes it to the right person. At least if it's marked for someone's attention, then there is an onus on that person to make sure that the letter gets to the person who should be dealing with it.

Exactly who in the department you should send the letter to will depend ultimately on the type of publication you want to work for. If you look through this book and find the chapter that relates to the publication you are targeting, you will see lists of staff on that type of publication and can work out who is likely to deal with commissioning. However, since even publications of the same type vary enormously, your best bet is to ring up and ask who you should send your work in to. Ring the editorial department, or the editor's PA, and ask who sports copy should be sent in to, or where your list of ideas should go.

What should it say?

The letter should basically answer the simple questions: who, what, why, when and how. Explain briefly *who* you are (including your writing/ journalistic experiences to date); *what* you want to do; *why* you think you're the right person to do it; *when* you think the piece would be right (for example, this seems to be a particularly topical issue at the moment – or, this would make a great feature during the World Cup); and finally mention *how* you're going to do it (this brings in your credibility and all the WUCKNUPA qualities that were discussed in chapter one). You need to say something like, 'I know several people at the British Olympic Association and have interviewed officials at the club, so feel confident that I have the contacts to write this piece'. Obviously, if you are enclosing a feature rather than feature ideas, your letter will not need to include this information. You might still like to mention some of the things you have done in the past, so that they know you are trustworthy!

The **tone** of the letter is of paramount importance. For some reason, people writing in to editors feel that they can be extraordinarily patronising. People who have never written a word before, and know nothing about the day-to-day pressures of putting a newspaper or magazine together, feel quite confident about writing to an editor and telling him where his publication is going wrong and exactly what he should do to put it right.

You would never write to the Managing Director of a local company and say that his company is useless and that you could put it right. Yet, to all intents and purposes, this is the role that an editor plays on a magazine or newspaper. So, be very cautious about slating the current writers or making destructive criticism of every area of the publication. By all means tell the editor why you think your work would complement the publication – but don't say that the current publication is useless!

You need to afford the editor some sort of respect. If you tell him that his newspaper is useless and should include your work, you'll make an enemy of him straight away and antagonise him so that he can't be bothered to take the rest of your letter seriously. Make sure that the tone isn't too critical. All editors like to be contacted and advised by their readers, but if you're sending a letter in and wanting to work for the magazine then you should remember that this is precisely what you're doing – working for the magazine, not taking over complete control.

Also, when you're writing your letter, mention anyone on the newspaper that you know or have bumped into at matches of sports events (especially if you got on particularly well with them). The editor may well turn to these people to ask what you're like, so that discussion about you and your letter will invariably move on a stage. It also shows that you are genuinely interested in the sport and in that particular publication, because you have been seen at sporting events and have made an effort to talk to local reporters you've bumped into there.

Every little bit of credibility helps, and editors will be more inclined to take someone known to their current reporters more seriously. It shows that you've been able to build contacts, and are enthusiastic.

Should it be hand-written?

If you have access to a typewriter, it is always best to type letters out. It makes them quicker and easier to read and shows that you are at least professional enough to have a typewriter (copy should certainly not be sent through in longhand).

If you don't have access to a typewriter then hand-written letters aren't the end of the world, but you will need to think about how you will file copy (write up and send in your features) if you start working. Chapter 13 will give more information on buying equipment; or you may be able to find a local library or college where they will allow you to use their facilities.

Other things to remember

- Never promise to do anything that you won't be able to carry out. If you suggest a great feature with Eric Cantona because you know his manager really well, you'll get completely unstuck and be very unpopular if you can't deliver because the truth of the matter is that you met Cantona's manager once at a bus-stop.
- Similarly, if you are sending in any cuttings, **never** be tempted to cut out things that you didn't write and send them. You can guarantee that this will be the cutting that the editor will pull out and ask you about – or worse, you'll find out that his wife actually wrote it. By all means make the most of all your achievements and promote yourself as much as possible, but don't tell bare-faced lies. If you haven't got the experience or contacts, don't pretend you have; go out there and get them.
- Keep a copy of anything you send – the letter, ideas, your CV, cuttings – so that you know what you have committed to and what you said about yourself in case you're asked anything later on.
- You could also put in your letter that you will phone up in a few days' time to see if they are interested. That way, someone somewhere will be forced to come to a decision because they know you'll be on the phone soon waiting for an answer.

What should you enclose?

You can put a CV in with the letter if you want to be considered for full-time editorial vacancies; but other than that, reference to relevant previous work should suffice. At the end of the letter you could suggest that you send in a CV if they want to see one.

If you can photocopy some of your previous work (just a couple of relevant examples) and enclose these, that would be valuable. Send a list of feature ideas including a fair amount of detail and make sure there is a contact number where it's easy to reach you. If the best number is a work number, make sure that it isn't going to cause you any embarrassment if a call comes through and someone else answers the phone. It may also be difficult to conduct a sensible conversation in the office if anyone else is listening, so if you have an answerphone at home it might be easier to give your home number. If they call while you're out you can call them back when you have all your notes in front of you, and you are in a position to deal with them properly.

Enclosing a list of ideas

If you have what it takes to be a journalist, then you will have what it takes to put together a list of ideas for a publication. If you find it hard to think of ideas then you need to train yourself to think laterally, and to analyse everything you read in papers more carefully.

As they read a piece, most journalists will think of a million different 'angles' for it. When you read a national sports report, think of the local implications. Study the area you want to work in until you know all about it. Ideas will then start to present themselves to you all the time.

Enclosing an article

Even if you send in an impressive letter and a list of fascinating feature ideas, an editor might well respond by saying that he's interested in the ideas, but would like to see the finished copy before committing himself – especially if he knows nothing about you.Therefore, if you have got all the notes together for a feature and have started writing it, it might well be a good idea to put the piece together and send it in as finished copy.

If the editor likes the piece and uses it, it's likely that you will get further commissions without having to produce the copy up front. If he's not sure about bits of it, he might get you to tinker with those – and your copy still might get into the newspaper eventually. If you'd just sent in ideas, he might well have dismissed them out of hand if they weren't quite right for the publication. Obviously, the downside of doing this is that you might put in a lot of work on a piece and have it sent straight back to you with a note saying that they're not interested. If they do this, it would be worth writing back to ask them for any comments, or ask them if they can spare five minutes for you to come in and find out where you're going wrong – at least that way you'll get something out of it.

At some time, when they are starting their careers, most journalists write articles which are uncommissioned and which never get used. Usually you will learn something from the experience if you persist and try to get feedback from an editor.

The next stage

Once you have written off to a publication, you need to give them enough time to consider your proposal – but not enough time to have glanced at it, forgotten all about it and moved on! This is a delicate balance to achieve. You want to be seen as confident and fairly assertive, but if you become pushy and people groan everytime they hear your voice you won't do yourself any favours in the long run.

If you put into your initial letter that you would contact them in a few days, then do ring up after that time has lapsed. The phone call needs to be very undemanding and extremely friendly; just ask if you can speak to someone about a letter and some ideas that you sent in. Tell them that you want to check that they were received safely, and find out whether the publication is interested in taking your work any further or whether any more information is needed from you.

If they say that they received the ideas, but that they haven't had time to look through them yet and will contact you once they have, ask whether you should ring back in a few days time. If they insist that *they* should contact *you* once they have come to a decision, it would be worth asking if they have any idea when that might be. You don't have to threaten them or tell them that there are hundreds of other newspapers that are interested! Just keep the tone of the conversation very light, but make it clear that you are very keen to work for them.

If you don't hear anything back after making a check-call, then you have several choices. If you told them that you would try again in a few days, then obviously you can phone again. The other choice you have is to write in again – perhaps with some additional ideas, some new approaches or adaptations to your original ideas.

If you sent in ideas originally, you could actually have a go at writing one of the pieces and send that in, with a letter explaining what you have done and asking for any feedback at all. Or you could re-send the original letter to a different person on the magazine if you are not convinced that the best person is dealing with your letter. Finally, you could phone in again and keep pestering them until you get an answer.

If you are determined and think that you are having an inordinate amount of trouble getting a response from the publication, then you might pick this moment to ring up and try to make an appointment with someone on the publication to talk it through. Don't automatically think that you have to get an audience with the editor for this to be effective. It may be extremely difficult for the editor of a busy magazine or newspaper to get even 10 spare minutes when they can sit down and talk to you. Bear in mind how many letters editors get, and how much time they would have to spend with up-and-coming journalists if they spent 10 minutes with everyone who wrote in. As a magazine editor, I can get up to 100 letters a week from aspiring writers; I rarely have time to read them all, let alone meet them all individually.

If you are told that the editor is busy, but the deputy or news editor will see you, grab the opportunity with both hands. Get in there to see whoever you can, and try and get any advice that is likely to help you. If you hold out for a meeting with the editor, you may find that you are waiting for a long time, and when you get there you may be given very short shrift. Even a junior reporter may be able to help you with some information and advice – it doesn't always have to be the editor.

What if you're turned down flat?

If a newspaper really isn't interested, and you have tried every approach you can think of, you have three options:

- keep pestering them;
- send in other ideas when they occur to you, but don't hassle them in the meantime;
- contact other publications.

The first option is unlikely to work if you really have tried to think of everything and continually pestered them; whereas the second option shows that you're keen. The chances of you hitting on an idea which they really are interested in are heightened with every idea you send. It will also demonstrate to the staff on the publication that you are keen to work for them and that you are committed and full of ideas.

The third option is obviously also worth considering. In fact, the best solution would be to send the ideas/features you have to any other publications that you think might be interested, whilst continuing to think of further ideas and maintaining contact with your first-choice publication.

Thinking of ideas

The biggest difficulty you will face when trying to get a break on a publication is continually coming up with ideas that are specifically suitable. This may not apply quite so much to a local paper, because as long as your idea has a strong local angle, it will be 'suitable' for the paper; it will then just be a question of whether they like it enough to want to use it – or perhaps a question of whether they have already used a feature like it, or have planned to do one in the not-too-distant future and have already commissioned it.

Constantly thinking of ideas and developing themes around which to spin stories and series is one of the most difficult things to come to terms with when you first start – but it does get much easier. There are obvious places to start. Newspapers will need stories that are topical, but not necessarily run-of-the-mill, you could get a fixture list of local sides and look back at the history of previous encounters to think of ideas. For instance, you may discover two brothers playing on the same day, or a man-and-wife combination. There may be a team coming to the area that your local side have never beaten, or it may be 20 years since a team last beat another side. Anything like that makes good copy, but you have to think of it first, so try to be ahead of the game. Visit libraries and read the national papers to get a feel for what's really topical nationally – local angles on national stories are always popular. You might think that the paper misses out on a key area: do they have a schools sport round-up? These are very popular because proud Mums and Dads will rush out to buy a newspaper if their child is in it. Do they have a team of the month award, or a local sporting hero of the month? These make good copy. There are often unusual sports to look at – underwater hockey, perhaps? Women's sports often don't get much coverage, and yet women buy a lot of local newspapers – and the editorial teams are often trying to specifically target women.

Look at local personalities, or national personalities who have a link with the area. You might even think that a 'Tried & Tested' series would be appropriate in the local paper. You could put together a list of all the 'odd' events going on locally, and offer to become the paper's action-girl or action-man and go around trying them, giving details of where you can play that sport locally. The recreation department of your local council will give you information on exactly what clubs there are in your area.

If your aim is to write for a specialist publication then you really have to 'know your stuff' to be able to sell a feature idea to them. Unlike local newspapers, which will have a sports department thinking about everything from football to synchronised swimming (and therefore will be much less able to concentrate on a particular sport), a specialist magazine will have a team of people who spend all day and every day looking at pictures of the sport, talking about the sport, and watching and writing about the sport. There will be very little that they haven't thought of.

The best way to get on board a specialist title – unless you have a USP which allows you easier access – is to start small and think laterally about what they need. A small team based in an office in London will not have access to local stories. They may well have local correspondents spread around the country, but if you can come up with a regular supply of local stories from your area you will find it easier to increase your involvement once they are familiar with your name and your work. Chapter seven will give you a greater understanding of how specialist titles work, but if in the process of writing for a local newspaper you discover a story which you think would be interesting to a national audience, it would be well worth sending it in to the relevant magazine.

The approaches to these two types of publications are entirely different and it's important to remember how different they are. Writing for a local paper, you have to take national news and work out whether there's anything interesting in it for local readers. However, on a national sports magazine or the sports section of a national newspaper you have to work out whether the stories you are picking up locally have enough appeal for a national audience.

National papers can be the hardest of all to crack. Again, the way in is to try and present them with something that's new and fresh. Your best chances of doing that – unless you have special access to information through someone you know or something you've done – is to look out for interesting local stories and keep pushing them through.

Getting a commission

Enough of doom and gloom and advice on what to do if a newspaper ignores all your journalistic advances! What will happen if they think you have good ideas and decide that they would like to run with one of your features?

The newspaper might ask you to write your feature and send it in on a casual basis: if they use it, you'll get paid; if they don't, you won't. Alternatively, you will be asked to write it in a more formal capacity – i.e., they will tell you exactly how many words you need to write, by which date they will require copy, and they may discuss with you what they think would be a good angle, and who should feature in the piece.

If a publication asks you to write a piece in this manner, they are offering you what is known as a *commission*. Some publications – not usually newspapers, but certainly several magazines and television stations – will follow up the commission with a formal letter or even a contract in which the various aspects of your spoken agreement are confirmed in writing. At this stage, the publication may also ask you to sign a 'rights agreement'; this is increasingly popular practice as magazines attempt to make money from world-wide syndication. If your piece is for a local paper, you are very unlikely to come across such a contract. However, if you move on and sell a good local sports news story to a specialist or consumer title, you may well come across this practice. Chapter 13 gives more details about the practicalities and implications of the various contracts.

If the newspaper or magazine does not mention payment at this stage then you might want to bring up the thorny subject yourself. If they say, 'We'll see what it makes', you may struggle to get any idea of payment out of them until you have sent in your copy and they have decided how much of it they are going to run and in what capacity. Unfortunately, unless you are full of confidence in your own indispensability, you may find that you have to leave it there and accept whatever payment they send you. Obviously if you really have a story that is worth something you'll want to push for as much money as you can get. Alternatively, put the story out on a non-exclusive basis to a number of publications.

Sending in copy

When it comes to submitting your story, there are several ways in which the sports desk may want to receive it: by fax, by post, on disk, over the phone, down the wire and via the internet are just a few.

Fax

If you have access to a fax machine, this is probably the quickest and most reliable method of submitting articles. You may need to check that they don't intend to scan the copy in (many scanners won't pick up words off fax paper or photocopied text).

Post

This is obviously the slowest method, and is rarely used by journalists. You may however choose to post your copy to an editor if you are also sending in pictures which need to be posted.

On disk

You need to check exactly what computer and software the paper is using, in order to establish whether you can provide them with a disk that is compatible. If you can, this is a great way to send in copy because you save them time in typing out your work once it arrives at the editorial office. Obviously, you don't have the immediacy of the fax machine – but if you get copy prepared early enough to allow for postage time, or if you live near enough to the publication's offices to drop it in there yourself, then you could do a lot worse than file your copy in this manner.

Delivering copy via the internet or modem link

This is entirely dependent on the equipment you have available to you. If you have the facility to send copy in this way, it combines the speed of faxing with the ease of retrieval from disk. (*See* chapter 13 for further details of what sort of equipment is available and what to look out for if you are considering buying it.)

By phone

This is the way in which national newspapers take copy, as well as many publications which need copy quickly and by tight deadlines. They have a bank of copy-takers who take down the words over the phone. If a publication asks you to file in this way, the most important thing is to make sure that you have everything well prepared and organised before you even pick up the phone.

Most newspapers who ask you to file over the phone have either a freephone number, or will phone you back to take copy, so you shouldn't run up huge bills.

Read out your copy slowly, and in phrases which will help the copy-taker to understand the sense of your feature – he will be less likely to make errors. Spell any complicated words, and any words that you think may cause confusion later on. Always spell out names, particularly in team lists; and make sure you adhere to house style, even though you may be under pressure on the phone to file as quickly as possible.

If the paper wants to know what time every substitution occurred, or where the referee was from, you must include it. Don't miss out details because the copy-taker sounds like he's in a rush.

Indicate punctuation as you go through, and finish each sentence with 'point'. For a new paragraph just say 'new par' or 'par'. Also make it clear what is going in speech-marks. Say when the speech-marks start and when they end, or you may find yourself attributing half your article to the coach, or whoever you interviewed after the match. Most copy-takers will be too busy to read everything back to you, but if you think you may have made a mistake or given a wrong spelling, do ask them to go back and check it. It's much better to upset the copy-taker than to upset the entire editorial department and half your readers with mistakes in the copy.

4 • TYPES OF REPORTERS AND TYPES OF REPORTING

This chapter examines the wide variety of writing styles and the very different writers that exist within the relatively narrow world of sports journalism.

When readers think of sports writers, they imagine them in just one role – attending events and commenting on them. In fact, there are dozens of different types of writers, experts, columnists and observers employed on a wide variety of publications performing an ever-expanding array of functions. At the highest level, sports journalism is an extremely sophisticated and technical business. Deadlines are terrifyingly tight, and sportspeople can be as difficult to get hold of as politicians and film stars. The old images of journalists sitting in bars and making up match reports for games they've never seen are now resigned to history.

In the past, some sports writers have rather offensively been described as 'fans with typewriters' because they have far more in common with fans than with 'real' journalists. There is obviously a role for this type of down-to-earth, non-investigative journalism (in fanzines and on some local newspapers), but there has been an enormous shift in the coverage of sport in the media, and editors today recognise that having the best sports writers and the most thorough, accurate and creative coverage can without doubt lead to increased paper sales.

For example, when the *Express* wanted to re-invent themselves in order to push their circulation up, one of the key things that they did was to polish their sports coverage – head-hunting some of the country's leading journalists, and setting their sports coverage out in a pull-out format in the centre of the paper. So there is no doubt that sports journalists today are taken more seriously than ever before, and top writers are invaluable to newspaper and magazine editors.

As sports have attracted more and more television coverage, so publications have had to think of new and original ways to compete. Today, newspapers and magazines are brimming full of different types and styles of journalism and there are many different types of sports writers around to fulfil these growing demands. This chapter takes a look two areas: firstly at the different types of reporting that you will be asked to undertake as a sports journalist; and secondly at the various sports journalists that exist – from those who sub copy on local newspapers to those individuals deemed astute and bold enough to write leader comments on the key sporting issues of the day.

Types of Reporting

Sports reporting falls into two clear categories: reporting the live events; and writing about 'non-live' issues such as the key personalities behind the game, the issues that arise out of live events, and the officials that shape and control the game. The covering of sports issues, politics, examinations behind the scenes, previews, reviews and interviews with the sportsmen and women are all vitally important to add colour to the sports sections, and bring both the sport and the publication to life. Many sports feature writers spend their working lives covering non-live sport, and indeed never visit a sports ground to see an event professionally. It is possible – though not necessarily advisable – to become an accomplished and respected sports writer without actually covering live sport.

However, most sports journalists enjoy being able to indulge in both areas of the profession. They revel in the competition and the immediacy of live coverage; and they enjoy delving behind the scenes to find out what the people behind the game are really like, and looking at the politics that will impact upon the sport further down the line.

The two areas of the profession require quite different techniques.

Covering live events

Reporting on live sports events is the reason that most people get involved in sports journalism in the first place. They get the chance to go along to their favourite club, to get in free and to watch the match, then at the end of the month to get paid for it! Unfortunately, like with most things, it's a little more complicated than this – covering live sports events can be extremely difficult.

If you are working for a daily paper and covering a mid-week match, or working for a Sunday newspaper and covering a Saturday match, you will find that the time-scales you are expected to work to are extremely tight. Most sports events take place on Saturday, so those poor souls who cover the action for the Sunday papers have the extremely tough task of filing the majority of their reports before the sports event has even finished in order to meet their tight deadlines. On a newspaper like *The Sunday Times*, journalists will have to file over half their report by the half-time whistle, and the remainder of the report through the second half – finally adding an introduction a few minutes after the final whistle.

There may be some time to do a re-write for the second editions after the event is over, *but* the first draft of your piece will have to be at the newspaper for around 5.00–5.30 p.m. If you consider that most sporting events are not over until around this time, you'll realise the pressure that the Sunday reporters are under. If you are reporting for a daily newspaper, your job is made slightly easier because your report will not have to be filed until the next day, so you have time to pull it all together properly in the evening before sending it in. Their tight deadlines come with mid-week games.

Procedures for covering 'live' sport

When you cover 'live' sport – whether it is the match or event itself, a news announcement or a press conference – there are certain procedures which you should follow.

Because there are usually people on hand to make sure that you get the information and help that you require on such occasions, it is worth finding out before you turn up at an event exactly what help there is on offer, so that you can make the most of the facilities and information available when you arrive. It may be a press or marketing officer, or perhaps even the club secretary or team manager. Before arriving, always ring up first and tell them you're coming and who you are covering the event for. Be sure to mention any specific requirements that you have; for example, you may need a phone, or access to players or performers after the event. They may not be able to arrange this for you, so you need to know beforehand and to make alternative arrangements.

When you turn up, you will need some form of identification such as your press pass or a letter from the club. For big events you will need to get press accreditation. This is usually arranged a long way before the event, so if you are covering a major sporting event make sure you contact the organisers straight away to let them know that you need to be considered for a press access pass. On arrival at an event, it is always important to be armed with the name of the press officer so that you have someone to call on if you need anything, or if you have any problems with access. When you ring the club to tell them you will be coming, always take the name of the press officer who'll be there on the day, and if possible speak to the person before turning up. If this is not possible, then make sure you introduce yourself to the press officer when you get there. This will make life much easier when you need something, and it will mean that next time you come to an event the press officer will know who you are.

Remember that as well as being the main source of your stories, live events are also fabulous networking and contact-building opportunities, and you should not miss an opportunity to meet and greet as many people as possible. Dish out as many business cards as you have, and aim to befriend as many as people as you can.

There are usually programmes in the press box that are given to journalists free of charge, but remember – **always** double-check the information in them. Many programmes are printed a long time before the match, and there are usually a couple of team changes or mis-spelt names on the team sheets. Run through the information with a press officer, and double-check anything that you're not sure about with someone after the match. Don't assume that just because it's printed in the programme it will be accurate – programmes are notoriously bad at getting things right. Remember that accuracy is one of the key attributes of a good journalist. If you spell a player's name wrong the first time you mention it – even if it's not your fault – you will find it hard to convince him of your commitment and credibility in the future. First impressions are extremely important.

After the sports event there will usually be tea or coffee laid on for journalists. Of course, this varies from event to event, but most larger events now have people working there who realise that keeping the press happy is vital for maintaining a positive public image. Many press officers will also provide journalists with a list of statistics about their club and members. These can be extremely useful, but remember once again that they should be double-checked for accuracy. Bear in mind too that they will have handed out the statistics to everyone at the event, so you are not the only person who will be using them. You probably need to think about using statistics in a different, more inventive way to avoid looking exactly like all the other publications out there.

After the event, there will probably be a press conference during which the captains, key performers, coaches or officials will come into the room so that all the journalists can ask questions. These conferences can be quite nerve-wracking events when you first start as a journalist, but it's important to use them as best you can to extract the information you require to write your piece. If there are questions that you want to ask, make sure you ask them as soon as possible, then make a note of everything else that is said.

It is usually worth having a tape-recorder at press conferences to catch everything. Your short-hand would have to be pretty special to get down every word said when there can be as many as six people speaking at any one time.

The difficulty comes if you have a really original, burning question to ask and you don't want the other journalists to hear the answers. If you do have a question like this then the press conference is not the best place to discuss it, and before the match you should have arranged with the press officer to have five minutes alone with the appropriate person for a one-to-one interview at the end of the conference.

The ability to work well at conferences, and to ask the right questions whilst refraining from giving away your entire story, is a real talent. Make sure that you go into the press conference with a list of questions, and don't give up until you get an answer. If the answer is evasive, and another journalist takes the interviewee off on a tangent, always pull them back in again and insist on getting your question answered – by rephrasing it if necessary, or trying a different approach. If you leave the press conference without answers to your questions you will end up feeling frustrated and annoyed with yourself later.

If you have difficulty asking your questions in front of so many other journalists, there are two things to remember. Firstly, it does get much, much easier with practice. Secondly, the key thing is to get in early with your questions before the conference really warms up and everyone is fighting to be heard. If you get your questions in early, you'll have more confidence to come back in later on if you want to, and you'll have your questions answered before anyone else really gets into the swing.

The sort of question that you will ask depends entirely on the publication you're writing for, and the article you are building. Chapter five explains how to put a sports story together. Once you know what areas you are interested in exploring in your piece, you will know what questions to ask. Don't *ever* let the pressures of a press conference put you off asking key questions which will accrue quotes and information that are vital for your article.

Covering non-live events

If you take a look at the sports pages of any newspaper, or the content of any sports magazine, you will see that there is as much coverage of the issues and personalities involved in sport as there is information about the direct on-the-pitch or in-the-pool action. There is more prediction, conjecture and discussion than there is pure description of events on the field. This side of sports journalism – the side which does not involve you going to a pre-arranged conference or event – is, for the purposes of this book, described as *non-live*.

Such coverage would include reviews of sports books, previews of live sport, and discussions of issues and politics in sport – for example, analysing the racism in sport. Most non-live 'feature' type articles arise initially out of the stories that are created on the pitch. If a black athlete is booed in a race, or an attractive female swimmer is wolf-whistled at, the reporters at the event will cover the story by telling the facts as they stand. Then, in a later article, there may be a follow-up piece on how this is becoming more or less prevalent in the sport, or a general piece about women or racial minorities in sport. There may be a behind-the-scenes look at the issue under discussion, or interviews with the protagonists in any debate.

Other non-live sports features may include lifestyle articles, which give colour and depth to sports personalities who are being seen as more like pop-stars or film-stars today, and articles about their lives at home with their girlfriends, wives or families make good reading for fans.

Another area which is being increasingly explored and exploited is the 'one-step-removed' feature. When Tony and Rory Underwood made the England rugby team together, most of the national newspapers ran stories on their mother, Annie, who was cheering fanatically at the match.

One of the biggest areas of non-live sport is the *interview*. Whether they hinge on a particular sports event, comment on an issue in the sport, or provide a gentle colour piece about a sporting legend, interviews are vital for giving readers a real idea of the motivations, interests and fears of their favourite stars. Chapter eight gives a comprehensive look at interviewing, but here are a few pointers.

- The techniques of interviewing are extremely varied, and hinge as much on the personalities of the interviewer and the interviewee as they do on the structure of the interview. You will have to vary your approach to interviewing in relation to the nature and personality of the interviewee.

- When you are planning to interview someone, it is important to think about what they will say. Of course, you interview someone to find this out – because they are part of a topical issue, or performing particularly well or badly – but if every other paper in the world is interviewing the same person at the same time, then you will teach your readers nothing new about them if you just follow suit.

- Always try to think laterally when it comes to interviewing people. If Duncan Goodhew is being interviewed by everyone because he has just retired, how about trying to get him together with another sportsperson who has retired – to discuss retirement in sport and what lies beyond it?

- Don't just interview someone because you ought to. Interview someone who will tell your readers something new, something interesting and something memorable.

- Preparing yourself properly before an interview is the key to extracting something interesting and useful out of it. Firstly, the interviewee will realise that you know what you are talking about and therefore take you more seriously. You will also be able to probe more deeply if you understand the subject sufficiently well, and have the background information at your fingertips to make a better job of writing the piece up afterwards.

- If you have kept a cuttings file, pull out all the relevant material on your interviewee and familiarise yourself with it.

- When you arrange a place and time for the interview, think first of all about what sort of piece you're planning to produce. If you want a long, in-depth character analysis of someone, you might want to try and meet them at their home so that you can include details of the way they live – their house, furniture and any family – so that you give colour, depth and fluidity to the article. Alternatively, if they have just been made skipper of the Oxford University rowing team, you may like to walk along the Thames with them, getting them to talk you through the race or to meet them after training so that you can talk about them lifting the boat out of the water as the sun sets and describe the scene at training.

- If you have a long piece to write, and you really want to explore the personality, then arranging an interview which has a theme can help give direction and life to your piece.

- Always arrive promptly for interviews. If you're going to be late through no fault of your own (traffic problems, for example) then always ring ahead to let them know – don't just turn up late.

- Most people now tape their interviews but it's always useful to make notes to jog your memory rather than having to play the entire tape back. I tape interviews, while making a note when anything particularly interesting is said. I also time all my interviews, and note what time a certain subject area comes up. That way I can write the piece from my notebook, just referring back to specific parts of the tape for actual quotes.

    Always ask the interviewee whether he minds being taped. It's unlikely that he will, but it can be quite intimidating if a journalist turns up with a whole load of paraphernalia and lays it all out on the desk without even asking.

- Make sure that you get the information you need from the interviewee. You may find yourself getting side-tracked into other discussions if you get on particularly well with them; but don't forget to come back to the questions you need answered at some stage, particularly if the person you are interviewing is short of time. If you go home without the information you need, you will make life very difficult for yourself when you come to write up the piece.

Types of sports journalists

Whatever the match, press conference, news announcement or event, there will be a range of sports journalists sent to cover it. In addition to radio and TV journalists (*see* chapters 9 and 10 for details), there will be the local sports reporters, national sports reporters and – depending on the size of the announcement – agency sports reporters and magazine writers. Writing for different publications is dealt with in greater detail later in this book, but here is a brief outline of who you can expect to see in the press box at major sporting events.

Local sports reporters

This probably sounds like the least glamorous of all the sports jobs around, but local sports writers actually get to the essence of sport – they cover a wide variety of different sports, meet lots of different people, and are able to get to grips with all the key local issues. There is also plenty of scope to write about national sports issues, since all national stories have their roots in local stories. Even if a national story does not feature a team or player from your area, you may still find that there is a strong angle for a local story which gets you an 'in' on the broader national issue.

It's hard work on a local paper; you may be responsible for everything from page layouts to subbing, writing and chasing copy. Hours can be long, and they are anti-social. Unless you cover a big area with lots of top sports clubs, you may find that facilities for journalists are either non-existent, or at best very poor. You may turn up and discover that there's no designated press area, so you are being jostled by the crowd as you attempt to scribble notes and have to contend with comments from the fans as they notice you scribbling and realise that you are a journalist. Obviously, many clubs have embraced the media, and realised that media involvement in their club is essential in order to attract sponsors, advertisers and investors; but if you decide that working as a local sports reporter is the way for you, it is worth being aware that there will not be many glamorous freebies and wonderful treatment along the way!

The benefits of working as a local sports reporter are that you get to cover a whole variety of different sports; you get to know the people you are covering because you're dealing in a small geographical area; and key people will hit the news week in, week out. This can be more pleasant and rewarding than dealing with completely different people for every story you write.

National journalists

National journalists will be at press conferences looking for a much broader, national perspective on stories. Their readers will be less interested in the local tittle-tattle than in learning broadly how the events impact on their lives. National journalists therefore have to pull stories into the mainstream in order for them to be interesting to appeal to a wide range of people. They will have to refer stories back to modern consciousness, pulling out issues that will be a point of reference for most people. As such, the questions they ask at press conferences will be very different from the questions asked by local journalists. They will want to know about global rather than local implications, and will often get frustrated at press conferences when local journalists ask about the specifics of an event or announcement – wanting to know every last detail about the people involved. But their jobs are quite different, so the two need to be tolerant of each other.

Agency journalists

If a big story breaks, the top agencies – like news agency Reuters or sports agency Hayters – will send a reporter along to cover the press conference. These journalists may have a specific brief; for example, to provide 250 words for the *Mirror*, 600 words for the *News of the World* and a 200-word piece for a local paper in Lancashire. Alternatively, they may just turn up and file copy everywhere in case one of the papers couldn't make it to the conference but decides to pick it up.

Obviously, agency reporters need to have very varied writing skills. They must be able to write in a myriad of different styles and under great deadline pressure in order to fulfil their many requirements.

Magazine journalists

Magazines tend to need greater visual impact and more depth than news-papers, who want the immediate news story for the next paper. As such, magazine journalists will probably be looking to tie up a match or an event report with a feature or series of dramatic pictures. Magazine journalists on monthly or bi-monthly titles know that they cannot compete with newspaper journalists when it comes to breaking stories regularly. Newspaper journalists will have a four-week advantage over magazine writers, so it is vital that they come up with something original. This often takes the form of a piece accompanied by fantastic photographs, because one advantage that magazines do have is that they have the facility and paper quality to run much better pictures.

Types of sports journalists on these publications

Subs

Who would want to be a sports sub? Surely the most thankless, if vitally important, job on a newspaper or magazine has to be that of the sub-editor. It has none of the glamour of meeting famous sportspeople, watching important sporting fixtures or waxing lyrical about aspects of one's chosen sport. The sub's job is to check copy for factual and grammatical accuracy, and to make sure it is the right length and tone for the publication.

The sub's job is *not* to completely re-write everything he gets his hands on, although many writers complain that this is exactly what he does! He tidies up loose ends in the process of making sure that the copy is the right length for its assigned place on the page.

Subs have to be meticulously accurate; they need to have good enough grammar and writing skills to be able to smarten copy up; and they need patience enough to check everything to the last degree (every name spelling needs to be checked, every date, time and the spelling of every word). The subs are also the guardians of house style – they need to make sure that everything is written in a uniform way. Some subs also get the chance to go out and write occasionally, before being drafted back to the subs bench. Sub-editors may have the chance to use their creativity on headlines, stand-firsts and picture captions – but most of their work is the excruciating task of acting as the last line of defence in checking for accuracy.

Columnists

One key thing that you are trying to do as a sports journalist is to tell people something that they don't already know. This can be extremely difficult on monthly magazines or weekly newspapers, when all the information has been broadcast on television, on the radio and in the daily papers. Therefore, many publications get round the problem of imparting new information by getting a new person to say it.

These people can be on the publication in the form of a *columnist*. If a news story breaks about the shocking amount of money in tennis, you will have read and heard about it all month, so you may not necessarily be interested in reading about it again in a tennis magazine. However, if Andre Agassi is a columnist in the magazine, you may well be interested to hear his views on the story. A magazine has told you something new if it can tell you how one of the world's top players feels about a key issue. It has added a new dimension to the whole story.

As a journalist you may well be asked to ghost a column written by a famous person. This is much harder than it may sound. You have the unenviable task of getting hold of the celebrity in the first place – usually a moment after he or she has played in an important match or participated in a major event. Then you have to sit them down and extract information from them which is interesting and informative. The celebrity will be unwilling to be overtly critical in his conversations with you, but your editor will want something fairly up front and on the record from you. You may then have to show the celebrity the column before you send it in, after making any alterations that he or she deems necessary.

If you have a particularly witty, incisive or somehow noteworthy style, another form of column-writing could be to have a column of your own in which you give your views or your insights about what is happening in the news. Columnists have to be creative and have hundreds of ideas; but they also need to be sensitive to public opinion. They need a certain style, really taking a stance on issues. If a columnist is good, then people will wonder what they are going to make of news as it breaks. If a columnist gains a reputation for being very 'anti-monarchy', then people will want to read their opinions every time a story breaks about the Royal Family.

Diarists

Much like columnists, diarists must let their personality shine right through. Diarists are normally journalists who develop a reputation for being witty and observant. *The Times* uses sports journalist Simon Barnes to write a Saturday diary in which he includes all the obscure sporting information from the week. His diary has developed such a reputation, and is so well-read, that people from all over the world fax him information about their particular sporting funnies.

Specialists and colour writers

The way to really make your mark and get on to a paper in the first place is to specialise, and without a specialism it can be hard to get that first break. Newspapers will pay for your specific knowledge of an event much more readily than they will pay for your irreverent writing style. Most journalists remain specialists, so that on national papers there are whole teams of rugby writers, cricket writers, swimming writers and athletics correspondents. However, if you show flair and originality, and assert a certain type of writing style that is fluid, interesting and easy to read, you may well find yourself being asked to go to other sporting events – even events you know little about – to write about the atmosphere, what the facilities were like, and what sort of mood the participants were in.

Your job, in this instance, is to add colour to the match report that will be provided by the expert. Newspapers will publish expert analyses,

statistics from the match and perhaps a column from an official or participant; but they will also use colour writers to talk about the atmosphere
before the game – perhaps to chat to the crowd or to a lonely police officer
about the event and what it has been like. They add colour, dimension and
a human-interest angle to the specific event analysis provided by the
expert.

Top colour writers can have a magnificent job, travelling around the
world to a range of different sporting events and waxing lyrical about the
day.

If you think you have the flair to write like that, then try to get involved
in pieces which allow you to express a personal opinion. Write 'tried and
tested' or 'birds' eye view' features – anything in which you can be creative
will help you to develop your own style. Remember to keep your cuttings
and to read the top colour writers and learn about their individual styles.
Think about the way they write and why they were employed in that
capacity. Could you do it?

5 • HOW TO BUILD A SPORTS REPORT

What are you aiming to achieve?

Even if you have witnessed the most exhilarating basketball match known to man, or done the most fantastic interview in the history of sports journalism, you have completely wasted your time unless you can convey this to the reader.

Your ability to use language in order to communicate information simply and accurately will be a key component in your ability to succeed as a journalist. This is not to say that you need degree-level, 'A' Level or even 'O' Level English – none of this is essential to make it right to the top of any type of journalism. And in a specialist area like sports writing, there are many other skills that are needed over and above pure writing skills. However, you will still have to establish fairly early on whether you have the expertise to convey your incisive thoughts clearly and accurately through the written or spoken word.

All the knowledge and understanding in the world will not help you if you cannot communicate well. That is why so many former players and coaches who dabble in sports journalism come to a sticky end when they try to move into the media. Some of them do it brilliantly, but many of them do it very badly, precisely because they are not used to having to communicate their technical and tactical knowledge of the sport in the written word. They may know everything there is to know about their sport – but their ability to express it may need some attention!

The good news is that you can develop your abilities as a writer by practising whenever you get the chance, and by reading everything. Never underestimate the value of reading widely as a writer. Studying other people's writing skills and examining ways in which other writers construct introductory paragraphs and conclusions is valuable in developing and refining your own writing skills.

Writing can be a difficult occupation, precisely because everything you produce is analysed and examined by so many people. The plus side is that you do get the opportunity to examine the work of fellow professionals, and this is of enormous benefit to you – particularly as a beginner.

Written work is around you all the time; every morning there are hundreds of writers producing new articles which you can read and learn from. Make the most of this opportunity to read as much as you can, both in your specific subject area and in other areas. The more you read and digest, the more ammunition you will have when it comes to your own writing.

The broad structure of an article

If you want your sports report to flow, the copy needs to be easy to read, simple and logical. Whether you are writing an aggressive leader piece that demands thought from your readers, or a flowing, creative account, you need to make sure that there is no clumsiness or careless construction which gets in the way of your words. For this reason, there is a fairly set structure for most articles which you can follow to make sure that all the facts are included and that your feature is interesting enough to grab the readers' attention.

When you read newspapers, you will notice that most sports reports follow the same format as other pieces in the same genre. Match reports tend to be roughly the same in style and structure, and have a similar tone and balance. When you are writing match reports, you want to capture some of the flavour of the event you have witnessed. You may do this through the pace of the piece, or in the adjectives you choose, but you also need to make the piece as uncomplicated and simple as possible. This chapter aims to help you avoid clumsy sentence construction, too few paragraphs and bad grammar – all of which can make the most interesting and informative of texts extremely difficult to read and understand.

The first paragraph in an article is the introduction, usually referred to as the 'intro'. This is often the most difficult thing to write, and it cuts many writers short before they have even started. Since some readers don't get past the first couple of sentences in an article, the intro is an extremely important paragraph – it needs to contain the real essence of the subject you are writing about. It should set the scene in a feature piece, or sum up the main point in a news story. With this in mind, it is often better to leave the first sentence until last when you are writing; that way, you will know exactly what the essence of your piece is when you come back to the beginning.

Many writers will put an intro on immediately, but come back and tamper with it at the end. The choice is yours. But the important thing is not to become too caught up in worrying about the first sentence so that you can't get anything else done.

The introduction – why is it so important?

The first paragraph of every article is the *introduction* – the hook to pull the reader into the copy. It is the hardest part of the article to write, but a good intro can captivate a reader.

The intro usually contains the most pertinent snippet of information that you have, so having a good grip of news values helps you to assess what should go into it. This seems very simple, but there's not always an obvious line for you to take – particularly if you are working for a weekly newspaper or a monthly magazine and the story has already broken. Unless you're right at the top of journalism, you'll rarely be breaking completely new, earth-shattering news to your readers. As such, presenting the story you have and making it sound as exciting and fresh as possible – with a strong angle in the intro – is what you should be aiming to achieve.

If you work for a weekly local paper and you have to cover a story which broke a few days ago, look for a fresh angle or someone new to talk to. For example, 'Friends of Danny Henderson, the Slough Town striker who tested positive in a drugs test earlier this week, have spoken out to *The Observer* for the first time about their traumatic seven days.' Remember that the introduction is vitally important to pull a reader in to your story – it works with the headline to 'sell' the article, whilst being true to the story.

How do you write an intro?

One of the best pieces of advice that I was ever given about writing introductions came from an old hack who had worked in the profession for 30 years. He said, 'Sit down, look at the information in front of you and work out how you will tell your friend about the event when you get home'.

If you watch a match on a lovely sunny afternoon, and the home side plays dreadfully and loses by eight goals – their biggest losing margin ever – and it is the first time that the team has lost in ten years, what would you say to your friend when you got home? You would tell him that it was awful, almost embarrassing to watch; that Slough Town had suffered their worse defeat in ten years and conceded a record number of goals. You wouldn't mention the weather, what you had for lunch or how long it took you to get to the game. You would be amazed how many people send reports into local papers which start with, 'We had a lovely journey to the match, and enjoyed a very nice lunch on the way...'. Then down in the ninth paragraph there will be a mention of the fact that three people died as crowd hooliganism broke out, and the players had to flee the pitch for their lives!

This is an extreme example, but it is important to remember that in a news story – or in 'live' coverage – the real essence of the story has to go at the top to pull people in. This is where you can test whether you have got the 'nose for news' that was discussed in chapter one.

A good way of practising writing intros is to read a newspaper report and re-write the story with a different angle. Or write about something you did during the day, putting different introductions on it and seeing which intro makes the story sound more interesting.

Following the introduction

When you have decided what the main point of the introduction should be – thus hooking the reader into your story – you need to expand and flesh out the story by rolling out the rest of the facts and relevant information.

Often, the best way to begin this process is to simply write down or to type out all the information you have. Get all your information down on paper or into the computer and proceed from there. It doesn't matter what order it is in, because you can easily change that – you need to get *started* and to eliminate the innate fear of staring at a blank piece of paper.

The biggest mistake that most aspiring writers make is to sit around waiting for inspiration. If you just start – force yourself to write something about the event, and keep going until you've got all the facts in front of you to shape into an article – then you can add your touch of inspiration later.

This is certainly not the only way to write an article; if you feel more confident, you may be able to see right from the beginning where the root of the story lies. But it is a great way to get started if you haven't written much before and find the whole process initially very daunting.

What next?

Once you've got everything in front of you, with your research written out and an outline of what happened during the event (and during any post-event press conferences or interviews) all written down, then you can read through what the components of the story are. Until it is down there in black and white, it can be difficult to assess what the most important aspects are and how you are going to put some structure to the story that is starting to emerge.

What should go in, and what should stay out?

Don't think that everything you have found out about a person or event needs to go into an article. Just because you know his grandmother's name doesn't mean that you should try to slot it in somewhere to show how clever you are. Just use the facts that are pertinent to the article you are writing at that particular moment in time. Any additional information can be stored away for future use, and used to build on for stories to come. You may even find that you have piles of notes and research in front of you, but you have to go back and find out more in order to get exactly the right material to do the job properly. Never be afraid to go back and ask a few questions or check a few facts. You will need to be eminently professional if you are to succeed as a journalist – so never be afraid of working hard to get the exact information which you require.

In order to work out what should go into a piece, keeping asking yourself questions about it. The five key questions that a journalist should ask himself are: *who*, *what*, *where*, *when*, and *why*.

Who, what, where, when, why?

The five 'W's are the key questions that every journalist should ask in order to ascertain the basic facts for inclusion in an article. If one of these areas is missing then it will give an empty feel to the article, and the reader will not be left with the feeling that he understands all there is to know about the subject.

When you are fully immersed in a subject, it is often easy to assume too much knowledge and understanding from the reader. Just because *you* saw the match and spent five hours talking to the players afterwards, this doesn't mean that your reader did! Give plenty of background information and, unless it is a specialist publication, explain all the nuances that may arise. By making sure that you answer these five basic 'W' questions in every piece you write, you will produce a more balanced and informative end result.

Who?

Sport is very people-oriented, so working as a sports journalist will usually involve dealing with or referring to people more than you would in many other areas of writing. If you work in legal journalism, or if you write about beauty for a magazine, you can become very 'bogged down' in the products themselves – beauty journalists write pages about lipsticks and skin creams without referring to people at all. In the same way, a legal journalist may discuss issues or legal case studies without having to bring any colour to the individuals in the studies – they exist as names alone. In sport, however, individuals usually play a major role in shaping an article: a footballer's goal wins a match, or a gymnast is caught taking drugs. Even when technical articles are written about a sport, they often refer to a specific example of a sportsperson with whom readers will be able to identify.

Therefore, including names of people in your piece, and making sure that you have spelt those names correctly and that they are appropriate, is vitally important. In a match report, always say *who* scored, *who* played badly and *who* shone. The people are the sport.

What?

Remember to include fairly early on in the match report, exactly what the match is all about – for example, 'in this Pilkington Cup quarter-final clash between X and Y'. In a specialist area, there is often a danger of not giving out the basic information just because it seems obvious to you (and it may do to many of your readers). If you aim to pull in new readers and capture the interest of people who are flicking through the publication, you need to state clearly at the top of your piece exactly what match, competition or tournament you're talking about. It might not even be clear what sport you're talking about unless you're careful to provide the basic information at the top of the story.

Where?

Make sure you include some details of where the event took place. Even just by saying 'home game' or 'playing away at Anfield', you will give information to the reader about the context of the story you are about to unfold. In sport, it is particularly important to let people know whether it was a home or away win because there is relevance attached to it in terms of the significance of the result.

In the case of an athletics meeting or tournament, people like to know where an event took place because in future it may well be referred to as 'the Brussels meeting' or 'the Stockholm race'.

Stating where an event took place lends colour and interest to a piece – such information is too often missed out.

When?

Even if you are writing for a publication which is not time-sensitive, you should still include details of when the match took place. Make sure that you remember the time difference. For example, if you cover a Saturday match and file your report on Sunday, do not refer to 'yesterday's match' if it's for Monday's paper – talk about 'Saturday's match'. The subs are in the office to look out for such mistakes as they occur, but it is important to make your piece as accurate as possible yourself, because mistakes like these do slip through. If you don't make them in the first place, then they can't slip through! You'll also be extremely popular with the subs, which can only help you to get future work.

The 'when?' question also refers to times of goals or times in races. Most sports have some timing element. Make sure you check with the individual publication to find out exactly how much information they require in respect of the timings. Some newspapers will want to know exactly when every goal was scored; others will just want to know whether it was in the first or second half.

Why?

Even if you're just writing a local report on a minor game, you need to answer the question, 'Why are you writing it?'. In other words, you need an *angle*, and you need to use it fairly early on in the piece. You must therefore be aware, when you go to cover a match, of what the implications are and why you are there for the paper. Why is the event important enough to merit space?

One way to do this is to give some history to the event – 'the fourth clash between these two sides, all of which have been won by Reading'. Alternatively, you can give the readers some idea of the relevance of the event:

- 'In this match, which could have taken them clear to the top of the league, ...'
- 'In this promotion clash...' (you are explaining that the match report is in there because it was such a crucially important game)
- 'With Sean Fitzpatrick captaining for the 10th time, ...'

Your own individual style

Although it is essential that you include all the basic information in any piece you write, there is plenty of room for you to be as inventive and creative as you want – obviously within the set brief and within the parameters outlined by the magazine or newspaper you are writing for. The other important thing to remember is that there are absolutely no hard and fast rules about writing, and as long as you get the information across simply and accurately, the style you adopt can be very individual. Indeed, on most national newspapers there is a collection of writers who are chosen specifically because of their unique approach, or individual style of writing.

The best approach is to 'be yourself'. This is worth bearing in mind if you find yourself copying other journalists' styles too much. All you do have to be wary of is investing too much of your own personality into the piece in terms of making personal comments. It is unusual for a newspaper to want you to rant on about your opinions in the context of an unbiased, balanced match report. Comments pages and 'speak out' columns are different. Beware of sounding like a fan let loose on a typewriter! You are a professional journalist commissioned to write an informative and entertaining piece.

House style

Every magazine and newspaper has a certain style. Some of the elements that make up this style are instantly discernible. The style of the newspaper or magazine will give you an instant insight into the sort of people that read the publication. You don't have to look too closely at *The Times* and the *News of the World* to discover that despite being produced by the same company, they are geared towards completely different markets; and that they establish these differences through their content and style. Clearly, the *News of the World* focuses its sports editorial on football, boxing and racing – the key sports that their readers enjoy. *The Times* and *The Telegraph* offer much more wide-ranging coverage to cater for their market, and include rugby and cricket – traditionally middle-class sports – to a much greater degree.

As well as content, newspapers have their own set style which helps them to acquire distinction in a cluttered marketplace. If a magazine or a newspaper has been well designed, and it falls open on any page, the public should easily be able to tell which publication it is by the style and the page layout. It is vitally important for publications to work on developing their own unique style, because by definition the product changes each time. The news is never the same twice, so all that remains to set one paper apart from another is style.

A publication is a product, and its publishers will be looking to promote it and to develop its branding at every stage. 'Style' makes one publication discernible from another and therefore allows it to be marketed as unique.

In terms of your input, there are guidelines laid down by the publication which help to give it a familiar 'brand' feel every month. Within these guidelines, writers may be as creative, individual and stylish as they wish. Most newspapers and magazines have these guidelines laid down in a style-sheet, so it is well worth asking whether you can have a copy of the style-sheet before you start writing anything for a publication.

If there is no style sheet, there may be key questions that you want to ask about the way in which the piece should be written: for example, 'Do you use first names in match or event reports?'. Traditionally, sports reports have included the first name of the player or participant when first mentioning them, then referred to them by their surname (without any title) thereafter. Increasingly, though, national newspapers are dropping any mention of first names, because in match reports so many people are mentioned that including first names can lead to cluttered copy. Your best bet is to check in advance what the paper's view is. There is also the issue of how they want you to file teams and scorers at the end of a report. Does the sports desk want to know what time the runs were scored or catches were made? Do they need times of substitutions? How will they list the race winners? Do they want all the swimmers' times? You can obviously glean much of this information from reading the paper, but it is also worth asking the sports desk. In the process of writing a report you will undoubtedly be referring to a lot of numbers, so one of the things you will have to check is how they want numbers written. Usually numbers one to nine are written out, and numerals used after that.

The newspaper may also have a view on whether they like quotes, opinions and observations to be included in the piece. These can add colour to a match report, but some newspapers think that comments from a player who has just walked off the pitch are worse than useless. If you are going to include quotes, make sure they take the story somewhere new – or at least add a colourful dimension. Many quotes just repeat what the journalist has already said or are mindless and should not be included.

Dividing text

All the words in your piece will be divided into sentences which would normally contain one fact. A series of sentences which allude to a similar topic or subject area is a paragraph. In many newspapers one sentence forms a paragraph on its own – this is particularly true with news stories where a concise writing style dictates that independent facts are presented one after the other in quick succession in separate paragraphs.

Keeping sentences and paragraphs as short as possible is paramount in most newspapers and magazines, unless you have the luxury of writing a long and lazy piece. In most papers, the object is to captivate the reader with a dynamic headline and first paragraph, then to keep people reading by rolling out the rest of the facts in the story as concisely and interestingly as possible. Short paragraphs and snappy adjectives can change the pace of a story immensely, making it more newsy and faster. It really depends on the subject you are writing about, and on house style.

Different types of articles

The sort of article you write and the way you structure it depends, to some extent, on the timing of the piece. Let's take the example of a selection of reporters at a boxing match on a Saturday afternoon. There will be a mixture of people who are filing their reports for the Sunday paper the next day, for the Monday papers, for weekly local papers, for monthly specialist magazines and for weekly specialist papers.

- The journalist writing his report for the next day will give a 'blow by blow' account of the match, for many people will not yet have heard what happened.
- The journalist working for the Monday paper will have to write less of a minute-by-minute account, because by Sunday the result and what happened will already have been printed. *His* job is to provide an analysis of the match, and to sum up what the implications are.
- A journalist working for a specialist title will probably want to put the match into context, analysing where the result takes the sport, and what the implications are. His report will be appearing up to six weeks later, so everyone will know the result and what happened.
- Local newspaper journalists will obviously reach for the main local hook in the story, perhaps angling their piece on the fight of the home boxer and talking to local fans and administrators afterwards.

6 • NEWSPAPERS

The role of sport in newspapers

Although news, politics, home and foreign affairs dominate British newspapers, all editors recognise that sport has a significant role to play in the content mix of any paper and so afford it a prime, regular site and treat it seriously. They recognise that many people buy a certain newspaper because they like the sports coverage or the sports writers.

Many of the national papers use sport as a big selling point. *The Times* and the *Telegraph* both push their Monday papers on the sports content, and when they tie a big sporting name or a top journalist into a contract, they are very quick to promote this as a real advantage of the newspaper. For although sport is a very visual occupation, and thus in theory much better suited to television, people everywhere still want to be able to read at leisure and at their own pace about their chosen sports. Watching sport on television involves viewing the action and listening to the comments at someone else's prearranged pace. Newspapers can be read slowly or glanced at quickly; they can be read anywhere – on the train, in the bath, at work or at home.

In this context, newspaper writers must remember that many of their readers have not been to or seen the sports event that they are writing about, so it is therefore essential to bring some of the life and colour of the occasion to the pages. You obviously need to let the reader know what happened in the event itself, but you need to do much more than that – you have to make sure the reader gets a glimpse into what the atmosphere at the event was like and what the broader issues were. Add some colour to the piece, and take the story on a stage further so that you are looking at the wider consequences of the match and what it means for the sport generally.

What newspaper you work for will determine the sort of report you produce. If it's a daily paper, then you will obviously be looking at a much more current angle than if it's a weekly paper, which needs to remain interesting once it has sat on the shelves for a week.

The national daily newspapers aim to cover the topical stories, matches and interviews in great depth and with great authority. Although many people thought that the arrival of televised sport, and all the instant access to sporting information which channels like Sky offered, would diminish the role of newspapers, this has not happened. Indeed, it has made newspapers realise how much sharper, more original and more exciting they have to be to capture the imagination of their readers – so that it has in fact made the whole marketplace more vibrant. Newspaper editors continue to acknowledge the massive role that they play in disseminating sporting information, and they work hard to recruit the most popular sports journalists and the best photographers, and to give as much space as they can afford to the subject.

Working for a newspaper is extremely hard work for exactly the same reasons that it is extremely challenging and exciting. Being the first journalist to break stories, filing match reports minutes after the final whistle and chasing sports stars from country to country in search of an interview, are all part and parcel of life as a leading newspaper sports reporter.

How do newspapers work?

Even though newspapers are up-to-the-minute publications that aim to bring you all the sports news as and when it happens, it's important to remember that much of the work does go on a long way in advance. You need, therefore, to come up with ideas for features with enough notice if they are going to be used properly.

Only 'hard' sports news can be taken at the last minute. If a team is going to be announced at 1.00 p.m., then you have no choice but to wait for that time before you can file your copy. Obviously, the same applies to matches. But if a club's anniversary is coming up, if there's an interesting angle on a news item which might make a nice feature, or if there's a new player coming to the area that you'd like to interview – let the paper know as soon as possible. In order to counteract the late news arriving, newspapers like to get as much copy in as possible in advance.

As a freelance sports writer, you may be a little disappointed with an apparent lack of importance attached to the work you've done. The sports desk staff always appear to be concentrating on the hot news stories that arrive on the day. In actual fact, without stories coming in advance and without freelance journalists who can identify stories and file them in advance, sports pages would struggle to come out at all.

The marketplace

Per head of population, we read more newspapers than any other country in the world. The provincial press vastly overshadows the nationals, but national papers still represent the dream for every young journalist.

Provincial papers

Provincial newspapers – whether they are local, regional, weekly or daily – represent the vast majority of the newspapers produced in this country. For a sports journalist, they are usually the first place to turn with an idea for a story or an application for a full-time job.

Most journalists start their route to the top on local newspapers, and many stay working locally – either working up through the newspaper to become sports editor or editor, or moving on to bigger or more frequent regional newspapers.

Local newspapers are obviously interested in local stories, so as soon as you contact them about any event that is happening in your area, you need a good angle. Because local newspapers are competing directly with each other, and not with other areas of the media, you may find that any local stories you pick up for your newspaper can later be re-written for the national papers or for specialist magazines (obviously after they have been published in the paper that they were originally written for). So by securing work on a local paper, and digging out big stories, you may find an in-road into a specialist magazine, or even on to the nationals.

National newspapers

National papers fall into two distinct camps, based on their size. The smaller newspapers are known as *tabloids* (meaning small), and the larger papers are known as *broadsheets*.

The size of a newspaper reflects the sort of readers that it aims to attract, because it represents a cultural as well as a physical distinction. Clearly, also, the difference in size of the two types of newspapers is a reflection of their style, approach, content and target audience.

The broadsheets

These are known as 'heavies' or 'qualities', because they cover events in a more serious way. This serious approach is reflected in the papers' sports coverage as well as in the way they treat news and current affairs.

In *The Times*, *The Daily Telegraph*, *The Independent* and *The Guardian* sport is covered seriously, particularly on Monday when the weekend sport is covered in detail (often in a separate supplement). These papers' correspondents are extremely knowledgeable and well respected in the sport. They provide detailed assessments of matches and detailed statistics, as well as analysing the outcomes and implications of sporting results.

Broadsheets are aimed at readers higher up the socio-economic scale than tabloid newspapers, so this is often reflected in the type of sports they cover as well as in the manner in which they cover them. The broadsheets still focus on football, but the traditionally middle-class sports like cricket and rugby are given more coverage here, as are events like the Oxford and Cambridge boat race, Ascot and the Henley regatta.

Tabloid newspapers

These can be divided into two categories: the middle-range papers like the *Daily Express* and the *Daily Mail*, and the 'down-market tabloids' like *The Sun* and the *Daily Mirror*.

Tabloids cover sport, but usually in a more 'titillating' fashion. They tend to look at lifestyle issues, and treat sports stars like celebrities. This is particularly true of the down-market tabloids. Obviously, they run match reports, offer detailed accounts of events and analyse games, but their market is different from the market catered for by the broadsheets.

They assume less detailed knowledge in their readers, and they run reports which will have as broad an appeal as possible.

Dailies versus Sundays

To work for a daily you need to be entirely professional, be thoroughly conversant with the issues in your sport and have a plethora of contacts. The Sunday papers may seem like a softer option because they only come out once a week; but if you think about it, they are actually much harder work because they come out the day after Saturday – the main day in the sporting week. In other words, they act like dailies for Saturday.

If you write a match or event report for a Sunday newspaper, you will have to be on the phone with your copy by around 6.00 p.m. Think about the time at which the average sporting event finishes, and you'll realise how tough the task is. Taking the example of a football match, the Sunday reporters tend to phone over the team lists before the match kicks off. They phone over around 300 words by half-time, and the remainder is phoned over 'on the whistle'. This is an extremely difficult job, made harder by having to call on a mobile phone half-way through an event, with all the noise and distraction of a live sporting encounter in the background.

As well as being the daily paper for Saturday's matches and other sporting fixtures, the Sundays also aim to summarise the week's sporting activities, adding a perspective to the events which is different from the dailies. They pride themselves on being distinct from the daily papers, so there's no point in churning out the same stories that have been appearing all week long. If the Sundays all ran the same stories as the dailies, they would eventually erode the need for people to buy a Sunday newspaper – and put themselves out of a job.

Sunday papers can be hard work for a journalist, but covering Saturday stories for a daily paper has its own unique set of difficulties. If you cover a sporting fixture on Saturday for Monday's paper, you have the job of making sure that your account is not the same as the one that appeared in the Sunday paper. You need some different quotes, a unique slant or a creative twist to make sure that your story is different, and you don't have the entire weekend in which to write it. Most Monday papers like copy in early on Sunday morning.

Writing for local newspapers

Getting started on a national newspaper can be extremely difficult, because places are limited and the stakes are high. Editors want proof that you can do the job before they will take a chance with you, unless you are a sports star in your own right or a 'name' that they wish to be associated with. For most people, the starting place is on the provincial newspapers.

Local and regional newspapers are often desperate for help with coverage, because their one or two members of staff cannot cover the dozens of events that need covering. You may not be paid at all, and you will certainly not be paid well for local newspaper sports reports; but they are an excellent way of establishing yourself as a writer, getting a portfolio and learning the tricks of the trade.

To start working for a local newspaper, you will need to get a fairly good grasp of what the locality is like. Which are the key sports clubs? Who are the sports stars? What are the stories that interest people? No local newspaper sports editor is going to expect a novice writer to understand the entire world of sport and all its permutations, but he will definitely expect you to understand the local stories that make the sports news.

Local newspapers vary considerably in size – from region to region, and depending on their frequency. As such, it is difficult to give broad advice as to whom you should contact on any one particular local. If it is a small weekly outfit, you may well be able to call straight through to the editor to discuss your ideas, or at least ring straight through to the sports desk. If it is a bigger paper with a larger staff, then the advice given in chapter three of this book should be followed – find out who the best person to contact is by phoning the sports desk, then write a concise, polite letter to the person who was suggested to you, and enclose either a list of ideas or a synopsis of a piece you propose writing.

Unlike the nationals, local newspapers will not have a bank of photographers waiting to be assigned their next job, and their sports desk may be keen to receive photographs to accompany a story – particularly if it is a match, or something which they cannot mock up afterwards. If your proposed article is about a person, then they may well want to get their own professional photographer down there to take a picture if they go ahead with the commission; but if you propose doing regular match reports of a sport which they have not covered to date, then you may well find them more interested if you can offer to take photographs to go along with your pieces.

Although this does seem obvious, the important thing to remember when suggesting ideas for local newspapers is that the stories must have a local angle. They can be based on a broad national story, but if there's not a local angle to them they won't be of interest to a local paper. To meet the demand for local news, you must be fully clued up on what the locality is like, and what sort of angles are likely to be of interest to the sports editor.

If you can think of ideas that have follow-ups, or that start a series, then you will start to make money from local papers. You are very unlikely to be paid enough from one-off stories, however good they are, to be able to rely on the money to survive. However, if you get your regular work on local papers, then you can start writing one-off magazine articles or doing pieces for bigger regionals or national papers, and you will soon find yourself getting suitable financial rewards – and, more importantly, **regular** financial income.

Writing for national newspapers

If you want to progress from local newspapers to the nationals, you need to make yourself known to the sports desk. The following are some suggestions as to how you might achieve this.

- Appear to be a real expert in your chosen sport.
- Make regular contact with the chief writer in your chosen field.
- Let the sports desk have your portfolio (once it is impressive enough to do the trick).
- Contact the newspaper regularly with feature and news item ideas.
- If you pick up interesting stories while writing for the local papers, make sure you send them in to the nationals.
- Make a real effort to network at any large sporting events. If you're there to cover the event for a local paper, look out the national journalists and introduce yourself. You can then write in to the newspaper in the future and say, 'You may remember that we met at ...'. Also, next time you're at an event, you may be remembered by that journalist.

Personalities

The national papers have started to develop the 'cult of the sports journalist' in recent years, working to promote their key sports writers as 'personalities' in their own right – personalities that readers will remember and identify with. For this reason, papers are often after 'names' or 'angles'. If you played sport to a high level, or have coached it – or if you can offer anything that will hook in an editor – make sure you use it to the maximum.

Papers do not like to take massive risks with journalists, so try to eliminate all the risks *before* you approach the national newspaper. Think through exactly what you have to offer (remember the WUCKNUPA characteristics discussed in chapter one). Having said this, don't miss an opportunity because you're too cautious! If you're confident that you have a fantastic idea, a good contact or a brilliant angle, **do** contact the nationals with it straight away. It is very difficult to get a break, so if you come across a story then use it as your entry into the world of national newspapers.

Once you're 'in' with a newspaper, you may get regular work covering your chosen sport. However, if you want to work in general sport features, or if you cover a sport which does not have a regular round-up, then you will have to continue to battle to think of feature ideas and send them in to the sports editor whenever you get a chance.

The important thing to remember once you get your break is that you simply have to do the job well, or you will find it extremely difficult to get any more work. Even if you come up with the best ideas, you won't have them accepted if you have shown that you cannot really do the work very well once you get it. A sure-fire way to upset everyone on a national paper sports desk is to file copy late, make mistakes or over-write.

Order of priority on the sports pages

The position of a story in the sports section can seem extremely important when you send in a piece. If you think you have got a good solid story, and then find they have tucked it away on the inside pages, this could be for a number of reasons.

Obviously, it could quite simply be that your story was not as good as you thought it was. It could also be a matter of timing or design. Unless your story is an absolute cracker, it could well be knocked off the back page because that page is being held over for a late result, or because an outstanding picture story has come in. The back page is a crucial site, and to a large extent it is the shop window for the newspaper's sports coverage. As such, a great photo story can knock a good story to the inside pages. Pictures make all the difference in the modern world of newspaper production, because pages are put together on screen and page layout is directed as much by design issues – what looks good and what will attract the eye – as by good old-fashioned editorial values. Today, with colour photographs, images beamed back from all over the world through ISDN lines, and all manner of creative tools, readers have become more discerning and are used to well-presented, well-laid out copy.

During the Five Nations championships I wrote a piece for *The Times* which went 'behind the scenes' with the England players' wives and girl-friends. It outlined what they get up to while the players are preparing to play. Even though it was very much a secondary, colour piece to comple-ment the main match report and statistics, it was given half a page and was run right opposite the main report simply because I had a diary of what they did during the day and because there was a lovely picture of them posing at Twickenham. Without the picture, it would never have been awarded such a prime site.

The back page is also usually reserved for stories which involve the key sport in your area. Ninety-nine times out of a hundred, that sport will be football. Sports editors will try to run a soccer story on the back page even if the story is weaker than a non-football story on another page, simply because football is so massively popular in this country. It may be that you will write for a local paper in which rugby or basketball are the key sports, and so they will predominate; but the main sport is usually football and there's very little you can do about this. You may feel that your tennis story is a really outstanding coup, but you have to understand what makes an outstanding story in terms of news sense. Unfortunately, a weak football story might mean more things to more people than a strong tennis story.

Newspaper staff

Whilst you will usually deal with the sports editor, or with the editor or chief correspondent of the particular sport that you are involved in, you may sometimes be put through to other people. If your story has a strong general angle (for example, sports and crime, or sports and race relations), you may be asked to contact the news desk. If there's a strong 'female' angle, you may be put through to the women's correspondent; or the picture desk, if you're being encouraged to set up a picture as part of the commission.

On local papers, things are organised very differently from on the big nationals. For example, on the first local newspaper I worked for there was just the sports editor in the sports section. He did all the writing, subbing, headlines and stand-firsts; he commissioned the photographers and ran the whole show single-handed. On the nationals, however, every job has one person responsible for it. One person manages the diaries of the photographers and assigns work; someone else has overall responsibility for each sport and dedicated sports photographers. Some of the key characters in a newspaper office are as follows.

Editor

On any newspaper there will be an editor who takes full command of the product (the newspaper) – of what it looks like and contains. The editor is in sole charge of the editorial side of newspaper production, and liaises with other departments to make sure that the newspaper is properly promoted, distributed, contains advertising and is making enough of a profit to continue its existence.

Although editors are protected to a certain extent from financial considerations, they do have to make the best use of available budgets and keep an eye on profits to ensure that their job, and the jobs of the editorial staff, are secure.

The editor may report in to the proprietor or publisher, depending on the size and the set-up of the publication.

The editor will decide what proportion of the newspaper is to contain sports news. This is usually dependent on the nature of the readership, but many sports editors have been known to complain when a new editor arrives who is less interested in sport and proceeds to slash back the amount of space allocated to sport. This is where the essential difference between working for a specialist sports title and working for a newspaper can lie. On a specialist sports title you all have one interest in common; whereas on a newspaper, you can find yourself battling for space with the news journalists who feel that their work is ultimately more important.

The crucial thing to remember is that many people buy newspapers for the sports round-ups. If you watch people reading newspapers, many of them pick them up and read them back-to-front! Never feel intimidated by news journalists who think that anything other than hard news is a compromise. Many of them probably harbour secret wishes to be sports journalists rather than to sit in court and council meetings all day.

Sports editor

The sports editor has control over the sports section of the paper. Depending on the size of the newspaper, he will head up a deputy sports editor and leading sports feature writers, as well as the correspondents for each sport.

Each individual sports correspondent will have a team of journalists – most of whom will be freelance – that he uses to cover matches, events and look out for feature ideas.

The sports editor has an important role to play in shaping the sports coverage, and in deciding how much space is assigned to a particular sport. On a national paper he will assign a certain amount of space to his sports-specific correspondents, who will then work out how best to fill the space by commissioning his writers to cover the key events. It is for this reason that it can be difficult to get things into a national newspaper by sending off articles 'on spec'.

On local papers, the sports editor's job can be very different. He will not have a whole team of journalists out there waiting to be told their pagination. Instead, he'll see what's happening and fill the pages with the best stories that come up. For this reason there is more flexibility. Often the sports editor will be looking for interesting stories as the deadline looms, and your suggestion may find its way into print.

Sports-specific correspondents and feature writers

Certainly on the national papers, most staff sports journalists are there because they are specialists in their chosen sport. Usually they have been offered full-time jobs on the nationals precisely because they have the knowledge, insight and contacts that make them worth reading. Breaking into the nationals as an all-round feature writer can be a tough business unless you are a truly great, imaginative, witty writer who is easy to read and has a real understanding of all sports (and you have to be able to assess this objectively as well as convince the most powerful sports editors in the country).

Some journalists cover more than one sport. They may cover football in the winter and tennis in the summer, or specialise in different sports as and when job opportunities come up. If you are third in line on the cricket desk and a job comes up as chief golf correspondent, you might well get it if you have proven your professional ability and your commitment to specialising in a subject. So it doesn't mean that by choosing one sport you are stuck with it for the rest of your life. It's just that in my experience, specialising opens doors on to the nationals – unless you have a real 'hook' by which to earn a general feature writing place.

Sub-editors

Whether you end up writing for a tiny local paper, or the world's biggest circulation paper, one thing is certain – you will come up against a creature known as the sub-editor. On a local paper, it may be the sports editor himself taking this role. Or you may find yourself working for a national on which a whole band of subs work, with different people contacting you every week.

The job of the subs is to turn the words you provide into an article suitable for publication in their newspaper. That's not to say that a sub's job is to totally change everything you write – far from it. The sub is there to check for accuracy, and to make sure that the correct number of words are there for the story to fit on to the page. Also to make sure the article has a suitable headline and that the picture accompanying it is relevant and captioned.

The subs know what the style of the newspaper is, so they will be changing things to pull them into line with the broad style of the newspaper rather than because they don't like them. If your piece does not make immediate sense, is cluttered or over-long, the subs will change it. It's difficult to get used to, but you have to avoid being precious about your words and accept that you were commissioned to do a job. You've done a job, and now the words belong to the newspaper.

Obviously, if changes are made which alter the story significantly and make it inaccurate, or in any way offensive, then you have to talk to the sports editor and make sure he is aware of your concerns. But if your only complaint is that the sub changes your work, then it is not justified. The subs are the guardians of house style, and when you accept a commission with a newspaper, you accept that the newspaper's subs will work on your words.

On most newspapers, it is the subs that actually design the pages, decide what type-faces will be used, and what size and style cross-heads and headlines will be. The type-faces will be fairly uniform, with the newspapers laying out what style they have opted for and the sub following well-worn guidelines. However, there is some flexibility and room for creativity, particularly in *headlines*, which are the real key to selling newspapers. The size of a letter in a newspaper is known as its 'point'. A 'point' is 0.01383 of an inch, which means there are 72 points in an inch. The huge headlines that scream scandal from the *News of the World* or *The Sun* can be this size for maximum emphasis.

The sub also needs to have a very sound knowledge of the laws of libel and contempt. Fewer sports stories land their writers up in court than news stories, but with an increasing number of sports people turning professional, it is increasingly easy to incur libel suits by effectively insulting people in their jobs. Linking a player with a scandal which ruins his name and may prevent him getting contracts in the future can land the writer in big trouble – particularly if it isn't true. The subs have the unenviable task of sifting through the facts, checking for accuracy where possible, and assessing which of them could lead to trouble.

A great deal of a newspaper's success depends on *how it looks* rather than what it contains. Particularly on tabloid papers, one screamingly good front page story can sell a paper, while a million decent stories inside will not. The value of a sub who can come up with outstanding headlines, pull the key quotes out of a story and sell the piece with dramatically used pictures and design is inestimable.

Columnists

To become one of this breed of writer you need tons of ideas, millions of soapboxes, a passion for your subject and efficiency when meeting deadlines week after week. The word count must be spot on, every time. Columns are harder to do than they appear. It is difficult to keep coming up with different ideas every week – but if there is something you feel strongly about, try writing a column piece and approach a newspaper with it.

NATIONAL NEWSPAPERS

BROADSHEET DAILIES

Financial Times
Southwark Bridge
London
SE1 9HL

Tel: 0171-873-3000
Fax: 0171-873-3929
Editor: Richard Lambert
Sports Editor: Peter Aspden

Daily Telegraph
1 Canada Square
Canary Wharf
London
E14 5DT

Tel: 0171-538-5000
Fax: 0171-538-6242
Editor: Charles Moore
Sports Editor: David Welch

The Guardian
119 Farringdon Road
London
EC1R 3ER

Tel: 0171-278-2332
Fax: 0171-239-9935
Editor: Alan Rusbridger
Sports Editor: Michael Averis

The Independent
1 Canada Square
Canary Wharf
London
E14 5DL

Tel: 0171-293-2000
Fax: 0171-293-2435
Editor: Andrew Marr
Sports Editor: Paul Newman

The Times
I Pennington Street
London
E1 9XN

Tel: 0171-782-5000
Fax: 0171-782-5436
Editor: Peter Stothard
Sports Editor: David Chappell

TABLOID DAILIES

Daily Mirror
1 Canada Square
Canary Wharf
London
E14 5AP

Tel: 0171-293-3000
Fax: 0171-293-3758
Editor: Piers Morgan
Sports Editor: David Balmforgh

Daily Express
Ludgate House
245 Blackfriars Road
London
SE1 9UX

Tel: 0171-928-8000
Fax: 0171-633-0244
Editor: Richard Addis
Sports Editor: Dean Morse

Daily Star
Ludgate House
245 Blackfriars Road
London
SE1 9UX

Tel: 0171-928-8000
Fax: 0171-620-1641
Editor: Phil Walker
Sports Editor: Philip Rostron

Daily Mail
Northcliffe House
2 Derry Street
London
W8 5TT

Tel: 0171-938-6000
Fax: 0171-937-3251
Editor: Paul Dacre
Sports Editor: Cameron Kelleher

The Sun
News Group Newspapers Ltd
Virginia Street
London
E1 9XP

Tel: 0171-782-7000
Fax: 0171-488-3253
Editor: Stuart Higgins
Sports Editor: Paul Ridley

Daily Sport
19 Great Ancoats Street
Manchester
M60 4BT

Tel: 0161-236-4466
Fax: 0161-236-2427
Editor: Tony Livesey
Sports Editor: Mark Smith

SUNDAY TABLOIDS

Sunday Express
Ludgate House
245 Blackfriars Road
London
SE1 9UX

Tel: 0171-928-8000
Fax: 0171-633-0244
Editor: Richard Addis
Sports Editor: Dean Morse

Sunday Mirror
1 Canada Square
Canary Wharf
London
E14 5AP

Tel: 0171-293-3000
Fax: 0171-293-3758
Editor: Tessa Hilton
Sports Editor: David Bradshaw

Sunday Sport
19 Great Ancoats Street
Manchester
M60 4BT

Tel: 0161-236-4466
Fax: 0161-236-2427
Editor: Tony Livesey
Sports Editor: Mark Smith

Mail on Sunday
Northcliffe House
2 Derry Street
London
W8 5TT

Tel: 0171-938-6000
Fax: 0171-937-3251
Editor: Jonathan Holborow
Sports Editor: Roger Kelly

News of The World
1 Virginia Street
London
E1 9XR

Tel: 0171-782-1000
Fax: 0171-583-9504
Editor: Phil Hall
Sports Editor: Mike Dunn

People
1 Canada Square
Canary Wharf
London
E14 5AP

Tel: 0171-293-3000
Fax: 0171-293-3517
Editor: Bridget Rowe
Sports Editor: Ed Barry

SUNDAY BROADSHEETS

Sunday Telegraph
1 Canada Square
Canary Wharf
London
E14 5DT

Tel: 0171-538-5000
Fax: 0171-538-6242
Editor: Dominic Lawson
Sports Editor: Colin Gibson

Sunday Times
1 Pennington Street
London
E1 9XN

Tel: 0171-782-5000
Fax: 0171-782-5436
Editor: John Witherow
Sports Editor: Jeff Randall

Independent on Sunday
1 Canada Square
Canary Wharf
London
E14 5DL

Tel: 0171-293-2000
Fax: 0171-293-2435
Editor: Peter Wilby
Sports Editor: Paul Newman

European
20 Grays Inn Road
London
WC1 8NE

Tel: 0171-418-7777
Fax: 0171-779-8641
Editor: Charles Garside
Sports Editor: Andrew Warshaw

Observer
119 Farringdon Road
London
EC1R 3ER

Tel: 0171-278-2332
Fax: 0171-239-9935
Editor: Will Hutton
Sports Editor: Alan Hubbard

7 • MAGAZINES

Introduction

The perceived beauty of writing for magazines is that it offers extraordinarily long lead times, plenty of scope for writing lovely prose, and the chance to be reflective and non-topical.

This may be true on some leading consumer magazines, but where sport is concerned, alas, there is precious little scope for you to indulge in any of these!

This chapter will look at the whole 'business' of magazines – their history, how editors go about putting them together, and who the staff in the office are. Chapter eight will then give more specific advice on how to go about writing for a magazine, including an outline of interviewing (the crux of most magazine writing), and of how you can get involved in writing longer features if you are creative and persistent enough!

Competing with newspapers

Sports magazines and the sports sections of consumer magazines like to be up to date, but they certainly do not aim to compete with newspapers when it comes to being topical and seizing the latest stories. They do have to work hard to keep up with the times, thinking of new ways to present information, new angles and new approaches so that when they are published monthly or even weekly, readers don't think they've 'read it all before'.

Trying to do relatively simple things like put together a magazine front cover in the middle of the season can be fraught with danger. Most magazine editors will be able to identify with the so-called 'curse of *Hello* magazine'. *Hello* magazine has a reputation for featuring happy couples at home with their children and dogs, then discovering in the next minute that they've split up and are no longer talking to one another! Similarly in sports magazines, the minute you put a player or athlete on the front cover you can be sure that he will be dropped, break his leg or retire from the game. Your cover-line will undoubtedly be really positive and glowing, making the whole magazine look dated!

The trouble with covering sport is that it changes all the time. With every result, every competition and every training session, something changes. You have to be careful of saying how many caps someone's got, how many races they have won or what their best time was, especially if the sportsman is in the middle of a season – because since you go to press a week or two before publication day and then sit on the shelf for four weeks, in that six-week period the statistics or facts that you quoted may be totally out of date. The way magazines get around this is to run several more 'open' pieces which are timeless. They may be a comparison of two swimmers in the past, fitness features or a timeless personality interview. This frees the magazines up to leave their news pages and more topical features or match reports until the last minute.

Timeless features

If you write a timeless piece for a magazine, you must be aware that it will often not be run in the edition it was originally intended for. If a topical news story comes in at the last minute, your story will be the one that is pulled. It may sit there, all designed and with pictures ready, for months until it is needed.

When I first started as a magazine journalist, the editor had just returned from India where he had done a feature on Indian children playing rugby in Calcutta. The feature was a timeless piece, so that although we planned to put it into the magazine month after month, it was the one that was pulled out time and time again as more topical stories came in at the last minute. It became so ridiculous that we would joke in the office that the Indian children would be all grown up and with families of their own by the time the piece made it into print. Unfortunately, that is the way magazine publishing works.

This sort of incident is much more common on specialist titles than on consumer magazines. On consumer titles they tend to work a long way in advance of publication, so you will not have topical stories coming in at the last minute and pushing your story off the pages.

History of the magazine industry

The development of the magazine industry was helped – like most industries – by an improvement in transport systems, and in particular by the development of the railways.

The new transport system meant that publications could be more easily moved around the country; but it also meant that groups of people were gathering in one place with little to do until their train came. Then, they were sitting for hours on trains with no entertainment. WH Smith were the first to take advantage of this, followed shortly by John Menzies in Scotland, both of them setting up stalls selling books at stations. This coincided with a government intervention in the mid-19th century on two separate counts. The Education Act was the first piece of good news for publishers – it suddenly meant that reading and the opportunity to access and enjoy the written word was a very real prospect for the majority of the population. This was followed by the abolition of taxes on magazines and advertising. The process of adding duty to magazines and newspapers became known as 'taxes on knowledge', and its abandonment meant that a public who were becoming increasingly interested in reading could now afford to do so. The publishing industry took off, and bodies like the

Audit Bureau of Circulation were developed to monitor the figures boasted by publishers and to ensure fair-play.

The growth of publishing continued through the rest of the 19th century and through the first half of the 20th, until paper prices rocketed in the Second World War. Unable to keep staff on when confronted with such extortionate rates for paper, publishers were forced to cut staffing levels dramatically so that magazines and newspapers started to fold under the pressure. The second big threat in the 20th century was the arrival of commercial television and its large advertising sales force.

It became increasingly difficult for smaller, independently owned magazines and newspapers to survive in this climate – they too needed the support and strength of a large sales force. As such, many smaller publications were bought by big organisations and brought under a corporate umbrella.

Today, many small publications are still in existence, but increasingly it is the larger publishing groups who own the real top-selling consumer magazines.

The differences between magazines and newspapers

We have already touched upon the essential time differences between newspaper and magazine journalism, and how this impacts upon the way in which you write and the ideas that you come up with. However, there are many other differences which magazine editors have to consider. The main one is *motivation*.

Motivation to purchase

Why do people buy newspapers and why do people buy magazines? This is an essential judgement for a magazine editor to make before he can begin to establish what promotions or marketing he is going to put in place. Without knowing why people buy the magazine, how can he create an image of the magazine that fits the desire?

The feeling in the industry is that many people buy the same newspaper that their parents bought, unless they are of a different political persuasion. Readers may alternate their purchases (i.e. always buy the *Guardian* on Monday for the media jobs), but strangely they usually go back to one particular publication for the rest of the week. This is usually the paper their parents read, and that they grew up with.

Magazines, on the other hand, are perceived much more as luxury items, and people don't see them as essential in the same way as they do newspapers. The motivation for buying them is very different, and as such the design and editorial qualities tend to be quite different too. Magazines need to have a feel-good factor about them to encourage people to make that purchase rather than to buy anything else. Research indicates that when would-be buyers go into a shop and start to browse, they may buy a magazine, a chocolate bar, or indeed any other 'luxury' item – it is the 'treat' value which gives them the inclination to buy off the shelves. This theory was borne out when the national lottery Instant cards started, and sales on weekly women's magazines slumped because women walked into the shop and bought a scratch card instead of a magazine! It seems illogical when the two are apparently so different, but the reality is that for these women the magazine was being bought as a treat, and the scratch cards were also a treat.

It is slightly different with specialist titles, where many are sold through subscriptions and people are inclined to buy them every issue. However, most magazines rely to a certain extent on purchasers who wander into the shop and browse before buying.

Types of articles

Whereas newspapers have to be led by facts and by the news of the day, and consumer magazines by trends and mass market appeal, specialist magazines can take a sideways or more obtuse look at their sport, producing a wide range of features to suit the range of people that are involved in their sport. You would rarely get fitness features or coaching articles appearing in the national press, except where they impacted upon an event that was topical or gave colour and life to a different story on the page. For example, if a runner burst on to the international scene and won Olympic gold in the 100m with a totally unprecedented running style, the papers might well run a feature about his strange running style, together with a separate piece about how you might improve your running style with training tips and fitness pointers.

The difference with a specialist magazine is that they might have a regular fitness or coaching spot, regardless of what issues are topical at the time they go to press. This applies to many of the features in the magazine – many of them are regular features that are considered important enough to the average reader to be included in one form or another every issue.

The following are some of the features you are likely to come across in magazines, and may consider contributing.

Practical features

These are the ones mentioned above: articles on coaching, refereeing, judging, scoring systems, playing, swimming strokes or anything that impacts on the practical element of actually doing the sport rather than featuring the personalities or officials behind the action.

Obviously, to write a coaching piece you need to be up to scratch on the sport and latest coaching techniques, and have access to the people who are influential enough to be taken seriously if you quote them in a piece of this nature. There is a great deal of responsibility involved in writing a coaching or refereeing piece, because you are giving advice which people will happily try to follow. It is important to be extremely careful – particularly in fitness pieces – since if you extol the virtues of heavy weights training you may well find yourself in trouble if teenagers (desperate to emulate their favourite athletes) take your unguarded advice and cause themselves damage in the process.

Take advice from the editor; but if the editor insists that he wants a point-by-point guide with no supplementary advice, don't be afraid to say firmly that you think this is a bad idea, and that readers need much more guidance than this. The article should be written logically, but always remember that you're writing for a magazine which has to look appealing in order to sell, as well as be entertaining and informative. A coaching manual full of in-depth articles accompanied by diagrams covered with impossible-to-read symbols, lines and arrows have no place in a mass-market magazine. You need to work hard to convey complicated and technical information in an easy-to-read, accessible fashion. This, essentially, is the crux of the job which every journalist does – but in the technical side of sport it can be much easier to leave all the hard-to-follow diagrams in, instead of working to re-write things in a more logical and accessible fashion.

Comment pieces

If the administration of your sport is in a state of flux – for example, if there are law changes or selection debates in process – someone on a magazine is likely to produce a comment piece on this. It could be regular columnists doing the work, the editor in a regular editorial slot, or contributors voicing their opinions.

The rationale for pieces of this nature is to provoke feelings in the readers. The readers are doing more than just digesting facts or learning more about a participant's character; they are actually being challenged either to change their opinion or to agree vehemently with the opinions being expressed. The features may influence readers to change their minds, or give them something to think about that they had never considered before. Whatever else the effect, they should provoke the readers into *thinking* in some way about the issues.

Writing like this may appear to be much easier than it actually is. It is simple to rant and rave about an issue, but much harder to produce a coherent, logical argument which forces people to think hard about their own views. Articles like this need a lot of preparation. Just because you are presenting your own feelings doesn't mean you can be offensive or jump to illogical conclusions any more than you can in any other area of journalism. You will need figures, quotes or anecdotes to support your theories if you hope to do a really good job. It's amazing how many articles which seem easy to write fall apart in your hands as soon as you start researching or trying to develop them any further.

Features

These are lovely if you like writing and enjoy having a little more space to explore a subject or a person in more depth. However, be careful to make sure that you have enough genuinely interesting information to justify all the words you're using. If you just fill the piece with adjectives without arriving at any real point, it will become boring and monotonous. Everyone has read a feature which seems to be so self-absorbed that the whole direction of the piece is lost. If you have 2000 words in which to write a piece, of course you can describe things at length and indulge in creative writing. However, it all has to be relevant, and it needs to take the piece forward a little for it to be necessary.

The key to writing good features is to plan them well – think about all the different areas of the feature, talk to as many people as possible and research it well.

Many magazines now want panels to run alongside big features, with sections in different colours or different typefaces to break up the mass of copy. They may want separate items, or ask for the information to be included in the main text. They may also ask you to get some 'pull quotes'; these are quotes that are pulled out of the text and used large in the centre of the page to draw the eye into the copy as readers flick through the magazine. If you can come up with some really punchy quotes for these, it will help the subs and it will show the editor what interesting information you managed to find. Chapter eight gives more information on putting together features and interviews.

Nostalgia

Nostalgia pieces are very popular in sports magazines; they are often the only sports articles found in consumer magazines. They can work in a variety of ways. Perhaps a leading sports personality talks about his best goal, best game or favourite player; or a journalist is asked to recall his favourite match. The feature may simply look back through the archives and take a different year every month to explore the past of the sport. Historical pieces and articles which compare the sport in the past with the sport of today also come under the heading of nostalgia.

The important thing to remember with articles of this nature is that they can sound extremely self-important if you are not very careful. Looking back at the past and waxing lyrical about its greatness only works if the readers know what event or person you are talking about, so don't pick something or someone obscure that no-one has ever heard of! Also, try to avoid sounding pompous and patronising. If you intend to look back at a great player and say how much better he is than the players today, back it up with facts or younger readers will feel alienated because you're slamming their heroes. They may never even have heard of the player you're discussing.

If you absorb yourself too much in an event which is in the past, readers won't follow along with you. Make sure you have chosen a particular event because of its sporting connotations, and not because it was a particularly great time in your life, or a particularly fantastic day.

Readers' views

Today, fewer mainstream publications let readers loose on the magazine in anything other than the letters page. In the past, though, many of them relied on readers to have their input and provide much-needed copy.

Encouraging readers to write in with their silly stories or proudest moments is fraught with difficulty, and the job of subbing them can be mammoth. Even if editors give strict instructions that no more than 200 words are needed, you will still get nearer to 5000 words every time!

The other danger is that people who are not accustomed to writing will fail to see how infinitely less funny something is when it's written down than it was at the time. It may have been great that they all fell asleep in the pub on a recent football tour, but if you weren't on the tour it just sounds like a rather dull story.

Match or event reports

These are obviously the 'scaffolding' of specialist magazines, on which colourful interviews and features are built. They can be quite difficult to write for a magazine, because if the report is being published several weeks later you need a new slant on the story to make it different from the papers.

These are articles that definitely get easier with experience. You learn what your own style is, and how you can best translate what you saw at the event into a report which everyone can learn something from.

Specialist areas

Even a specialist sports magazine will have different sections for different types of readers – a World section or a Scottish section, as well as women's, youth or schools pages.

These can be good pages to get involved in when you are first starting out in magazines. They do not have any of the glamour of doing an interview with a leading personality, but the beauty of them is that they are there every month so you may get regular work through them. You may even think of an area which should be included but which isn't at present. Working on one of these sections gives you an 'in' into the magazine, gets your name known, and may lead on to bigger and better things.

Consumer versus specialist?

Consumer is the word used to describe mainstream, general interest titles like *Marie Claire*, *GQ*, *Vogue* and *Cosmopolitan*. Obviously, the sports content of the women's glossies is negligible, but you should not rule them out. If you can think of a feature which falls within their brief they may well commission it, and getting a feature into a magazine like this means it will be well-designed and look great in your portfolio. They also pay better than small specialist sports publications.

You could approach a magazine and suggest that they include a sports update. This might address what has happened in the month just gone (very difficult to do with monthly magazine deadlines, because you'll find that in actual fact you are reviewing what happened about three months ago) or what is coming up in the next month. A women's glossy may not think much of this idea but a GQ-type magazine might. On a women's magazine you may offer to do a series of features on women in traditionally masculine sports, or a feature on how playing sport keeps you fit and which sportsmen are the fittest.

You need to read the publication first, but if you think about the sort of readers they are targeting you will usually find yourself able to come up with dozens of feature ideas which would sit comfortably in it.

Specialist magazines specialise in a sport, and they are a great place to try and place articles. You do have to remember that the staff are spending all day, every day concentrating on just one sport so they will already have thought of many of the ideas you come up with. Think laterally and work to come up with ideas which are original and will not have been thought of before.

Contributing to one of the specialist areas or sections on the magazine can be a great way to get started. Perhaps you live in the north east and the magazine has a regional section – get involved in sending in all sorts of little local stories until one of them makes it. Or look out what's happening in the women's or youth branches of your sport – there will be some interesting stories there that the editorial team will just have been too busy to uncover.

A magazine editor is eager for all the pages in the title to be as lively and informative as possible; but inevitably, the bigger features get more time spent on them than the smaller, newsy items. In actual fact it is sometimes that smaller, bite-sized story that readers are most interested in. Editors also recognise that having good people working on all areas of the title is paramount for its editorial success.

So someone who is eager to contribute to these less glamorous pages may find it much easier to get an 'in' into the magazine.

How are magazines put together?

The process for putting a magazine together varies from magazine to magazine, depending on the size of the team and the size of the publishing house. Most editors rely on a *flat plan* to organise their pages. The flat plan is an A3-sized piece of paper which is divided up into around 200 squares. Every square is numbered, and each represents a page in the magazine. The editor has to go through the flat plan and mark down which feature will go on which page.

This is where the fights with the advertising department really start. The most crucial advertising and editorial sites are the right-hand pages at the front of the publication. These sell for more money to advertisers, but editors are reluctant to give them up because if readers flicking through the magazine only see adverts they will be very unlikely to purchase. In the end, a balance has to be struck between the two departments. The flat plan belongs to the editor, but he knows it is important to work closely with the advertising manager to ensure that both advertisers and readers are kept happy. Once all the ad sites are marked on to the flat plan along with the regular editorial spots (the letters page, contents page and columnists will tend to be in the same place every week to give continuity to the publication), then the features have to be distributed.

Obviously there will be one main, key feature which sits at the front of the magazine and is usually the cover story (a picture connected to the story will be on the cover). For the other features, bear in mind that sections of the magazine go down to the printer at different times; so if you are intending to cover matches or want to wait until after a key event before interviewing an athlete, then you have to consider this when working out what page the feature is going on.

It can be a feat of enormous proportions to get all the articles down on to paper in the right order with the advertising department happy and all the main events of the day covered. As a freelancer, every time you are late in with copy the editor may have to move a feature on the flat plan to enable him to send off a section on time. This can be extremely annoying, which is why editors build in a certain amount of leeway into the deadline dates they give you. If you want to get on with an editorial team, make sure you get your work in as soon as you can.

Magazine staff

Consumer titles tend to have a bigger circulation than specialist magazines, so they can afford to have more staff. An average specialist title has a very small team of people and a large pool of freelance journalists and photographers working for them. They will tend to have correspondents in key areas of the sport and in key areas of the country, as well as designated people all over the world acting as correspondents for their country if the magazine is international.

In the office there is likely to be an editor who has the ultimate say over what appears in the publication. He will get involved in all areas of the magazine, often writing features, replying to readers' letters and writing the editorial, in addition to flat-planning, controlling budgets and being the public face of the magazine.

Below the editor there is usually a deputy who acts as day-to-day manager of the editorial team. If there is no dedicated commissioning editor, the editor and the deputy will commission features; they will also make sure photographers and journalists get their work in on time. It is often the deputy who has the rather laborious job of putting together all the news bits and pieces and the 'page furniture' like boxes of information.

Next in line come the features editor (not all magazines have one) and the chief sub or production editor. The role of the features editor varies a great deal, but it may involve writing, coming up with story ideas, helping with commissioning and assisting the deputy editor. The production editor liaises with the printers and the repro house to make sure that all the pages sent down to them are being printed properly and everything is running smoothly. On a small magazine the production editor and chief sub will be the same person. The chief sub puts headlines on to articles, picture captions, and cross-heads and checks the copy for any breaches of house style – or indeed, of the law! Having a good, meticulous sub is vital, particularly in a specialist title which is being read by real fans who will notice every little mistake.

A designer completes the package for a small team. It is his job to create the pages using the words, pictures, diagrams and tables given to him. Many designers or art directors also go along to photo shoots and over-see the pictures to make sure they are exactly what is needed for the magazine. It is useful if a designer can do this, in order to ensure that he has exactly the right material to work with and so can produce the perfect pages which the editor needs.

Photos and design

The main distinction between writing for a magazine and writing for a newspaper is that magazines are very picture heavy, and require a great deal more artistic input than newspapers. They are really led by images rather than words, so that if there is not a great picture to accompany a story then the story will often be cut down and used as a filler on a news page rather than standing up in its own right.

The designer needs to be given the right materials with which to create the pages, so if you – as a freelancer – come up with a good idea for a feature, it would be worth thinking of the merit of that piece in terms of how it will look on the page. If it can't be illustrated and the designer thinks it will fall flat, it may be binned unless it is a great feature idea. Indeed, you may find that the very reason they have not used the feature idea before is that it does not work well in a magazine.

ADDRESSES OF SPECIALIST
SPORTS MAGAZINES

Amateur Golf
129A High Street
Dovercourt
Harwich
Essex
CO12 3AX

Editor: Paul Baxter
Tel: 01255-507526
Fax: 01255-508483

Anglers Mail
IPC Magazines
Kings Reach Tower
Stamford Street
London
SE1 9LS

Editor: Roy Westwood
Tel: 0171-261 5778
Fax: 0171-261 6016

Angling Times
Bretton Court
Bretton
Peterborough
Cambridgeshire
PE3 8DZ

Editor: Keith Higginbottom
Tel: 01733-266222
Fax: 01733-265515

Athletics Weekly
Bretton Court
Bretton
Peterborough
Cambridgeshire
PE3 8DZ

Editor: Nigel Walsh
Tel: 01733-261144
Fax: 01733-465206

Autocar
38–42 Hampton Road
Teddington
Middlesex
TW11 OJE

Editor: Michael Harvey
Tel: 0181-943 5013
Fax: 0181-943 5653

Badminton
Connect Sports
14 Woking Road
Cheadle
Hulme
Cheshire
SK8 6NZ

Editor: William Kings
Tel: 0161-486 6159
Fax: 0161-486 6159

Bowls International
Key Publishing Ltd
PO BOX 100
Stamford
Lincolnshire
PE9 1XQ

Editor: Melvyn Beck
Tel: 01780-55131
Fax: 01780-57261

Climber
7th Floor
The Plaza Tower
East Kilbride
Glasgow
G74 1LW

Editor: Tom Prentice
Tel: 01355-246444
Fax: 01355-263013

Country Sports
59 Kennington Road
London
SE1 7PZ

Editor: Graham Downing
Tel: 0171-928 4742
Fax: 0171-620 1401

Country Walking
Bretton Court
Bretton
Peterborough
Cambridgeshire
PE3 8DZ

Editor: Lynne Maxwell
Tel: 01733-264666
Fax: 01733-261984

Cycle Sport
Kings Reach Tower
Stamford Street
London
SE1 9LS

Editor: Andrew Sutcliffe
Tel: 0171-261 5588
Fax: 0171-261 5758

The Cricketer International
Third Street
Langton Green
Tunbridge Wells
Kent
TN3 OEN

Editor: Peter Perchard
Tel: 01892-862551
Fax: 01892-863755

Cycling Today
67–71 Goswell Road
London
EC1V 7EN

Editor: Jerome Smail
Tel: 0171-410 9410
Fax: 0171-410 9440

Cycling Weekly
Kings Reach Tower
Stamford Street
London
SE1 9LS

Editor: Andrew Sutcliffe
Tel: 0171-261 5588
Fax: 0171-261 5758

Darts World
9 Kelsey Park Road
Beckenham
Kent
BR3 6LH

Editor: A J Wood
Tel: 0181-650 6580
Fax: 0181-650 2534

Dirt Bike Rider
PO Box 100
Stamford
Lincolnshire
PE9 1XQ

Editor: Roddy Brookes
Tel: 01780-55131
Fax: 01780-57261

Diver
55 High Street
Teddington
Middlesex
TW11 8HA

Editor: Bernard Eaton
Tel: 0181-943 4288
Fax: 0181-943 4312

Eventing
Kings Reach Tower
Stamford Street
London
SE1 9LS

Editor: Kate Green
Tel: 0171-261 5388
Fax: 0171-261 5429

Football Monthly
Prosport Media
Suite 108
Vanguard House
Dewsbury Road
Leeds
West Yorkshire
LS11 5DD

Editor: Steven Angelsey
Tel: 0113-244 3417
Fax: 0113-234 6243

Golf Monthly
Kings Reach Tower
Stamford Street
London
SE1 9LS

Editor: Colin Callander
Tel: 0171-261 7237
Fax: 0171-261 7240

Golf Weekly
Bretton Court
Bretton
Peterborough
Cambridgeshire
PE3 8DZ

Editor: Bob Warters
Tel: 01733-264666
Fax: 01733-267198

Golf World
Advance House
37 Millharbour
London
E14 9TX

Editor: David Clarke
Tel: 0171-538 1031
Fax: 0171-538 4106

Good Ski Guide
91 High Street
Esher
Surrey
KT10 9QD

Editor: John Hill
Tel: 01372-468140
Fax: 01372-470765

Horse & Hound
Kings Reach Tower
Stamford Street
London
SE1 9LS

Editor: Arnold Garvey
Tel: 0171-261 6315
Fax: 0171-261 5429

Horse & Rider
Haslemere House
Lower Street
Haslemere
Surrey
GU27 2PE

Editor: Alison Bridge
Tel: 01428-651551
Fax: 01428-653888

Ninety Minutes
IPC Magazines
Kings Reach Tower
Stamford Street
London
SE1 9LS

Editor: Eleanor Levy
Tel: 0171-261 7617
Fax: 0171-261 7474

Rambling Today
1–5 Wandsworth Road
London
SW8 2XX

Editor: Annabelle Birchall
Tel: 0171-582 6878
Fax: 0171-587 3799

Riding
2 West Street
Bourne
Lincolnshire
PE10 9NE

Editor: Amanda Stevenson
Tel: 01778-393747
Fax: 01778-425453

Rugby News
8 Peartree Street
London
EC1V 3SB

Editor: Graeme Gillespie
Tel: 0171-251 8665
Fax: 0171-608 3035

Rugby World
Kings Reach Tower
Stamford Street
London
SE1 9LS

Editor: Alison Kervin
Tel: 0171-261 6830
Fax: 0171-261 5419

Runner's World
7–10 Chandos Street
London
W1M OAD

Editor: Steven Seaton
Tel: 0171-291 6000
Fax: 0171-291 6080

Sea Angler
Bretton Court
Bretton
Peterborough
Cambridgeshire
PE3 8DZ

Editor: Mel Russ
Tel: 01733-264666
Fax: 01733-261984

Scottish Golfer
The Cottage
181A Whitehouse Road
Edinburgh
EH14 6BY

Editor: Martin Dempster
Tel: 0131-339 7546
Fax: 0131-339 1169

Scottish Rugby Magazine
11 Dock Place
Leith
Edinburgh
EH6 6LU

Editor: Kevin Ferrie
Tel: 0131-554 0540
Fax: 0131-554 0482

Shoot
Kings Reach Tower
Stamford Street
London
SE1 9LS

Editor: David Smith
Tel: 0171-261 6287
Fax: 0171-261 6019

Shooting Times
Kings Reach Tower
Stamford Street
London
SE1 9LS

Editor: John Gregson
Tel: 0171-261 6180
Fax: 0171-261 7179

**The Skier and
Snowboarder Magazine**
48 London Road
Sevenoaks
Kent
TN13 1AP

Editor: Frank Baldwin
Tel: 01732-743644
Fax: 01732-743647

Snooker Scene
Cavalier House
202 Hagley Road
Edgbaston
Birmingham
B16 9PQ

Editor: Clive Everton
Tel: 0121-454 2931
Fax: 0121-452 1822

Sport Magazine
The Sports Council
16 Upper Woburn Place
London
WC1H OQP

Editor: Louise Fyfe
Tel: 0171-388 1277
Fax: 0171-383 0273

The Sporting Life
1 Canada Square
Canary Wharf
London
E14 5AP

Editor: Tom Clarke
Tel: 0171-293 3029
Fax: 0171-293 3758

Squash Player
460 Bath Road
Longford
Middlesex
UB7 0EB

Editor: Ian McKenzie
Tel: 01753-775511
Fax: 01753-775512

Superbike Magazine
Link House
Dingwall Avenue
Croydon
Surrey
CR9 2TA

Editor: Grant Leonard
Tel: 0181-686 2599
Fax: 0181-781 1164

Swimming Times
Harold Fern House
Derby Square
Loughborough
Leicestershire
LE11 0AL

Editor: P Hassall
Tel: 01509-234433
Fax: 01509-235049

Tennis World
Presswatch Ltd
The Spendlove Centre
Enstone Road
Charlbury
Oxford
OX7 3PQ

Editor: Alastair McIver
Tel: 01608-811446

Today's Golfer
Bretton Court
Bretton
Peterborough
Cambridgeshire
PE3 8DZ

Editor: Neil Pope
Tel: 01733-264666
Fax: 01733-267198

Today's Runner
Bretton Court
Bretton
Peterborough
Cambridgeshire
PE3 8DZ

Editor: Victoria Tebbs
Tel: 01733-264666
Fax: 01733-267198

Trail Walker
Bretton Court
Bretton
Peterborough
Cambridgeshire
PE3 8DZ

Editor: David Ogle
Tel: 01733-264666
Fax: 01733-261984

Trout Fisherman
Bretton Court
Bretton
Peterborough
Cambridgeshire
PE3 8DZ

Editor: Chris Dawn
Tel: 01733-264666
Fax: 01733-263294

Wisden Cricket Monthly
6 Beech Lane
Guildford
Surrey
GU2 5ES

Editor: David Frith
Tel: 01483-32573
Fax: 01483-33153

World Fishing
Royston House
Caroline Park
Edinburgh
EH5 1QJ

Editor: Martin Gill
Tel: 0131-551 2942
Fax: 0131-551 2938

World Bowls
22–26 Market Road
London
N7 9PW

Editor: Keith Hale
Tel: 0171-607 8585
Fax: 0171-700 1408

World Soccer
Kings Reach Tower
Stamford Street
London
SE1 9LS

Editor: Keir Radnedge
Tel: 0171-261 5737
Fax: 0171-261 7474

Yachting Monthly
Kings Reach Tower
Stamford Street
London
SE1 9LS

Editor: Geoff Pack
Tel: 0171-261 6040
Fax: 0171-261 7555

Yachting World
Kings Reach Tower
Stamford Street
London
SE1 9LS

Editor: Andrew Bray
Tel: 0171-261 6800
Fax: 0171-261 6818

8 • A MATTER OF STYLE – MAGAZINE FEATURES AND INTERVIEWING

Feature articles are very different from news stories. When an editor commissions you to write 2000 words; initially it can seem extremely daunting. In fact, once you get some experience under your belt, you'll find that having the extra words is much more of a bonus than a burden because it gives you the opportunity to explore the subject matter properly. This chapter takes a look at the whole issue of magazine style, including some of the grammatical techniques that you can employ to make sure your pieces flow smoothly and comfortably. There is also a sample of a sports magazine style-sheet, page 89, which should help to give you an idea of how magazines like you to write. Finally, the chapter takes an in-depth look at the process of interviewing which so often forms the pivot of magazine features.

Putting a feature together

Most magazine journalists work on computers, since putting 2000-word features together in a note-book then typing them out can be extremely laborious. However, even if you have access to a computer, remember that you must still plan properly – as if you were having to construct the article on paper. It is foolish to rely on the fact that you can easily get all the words down on the computer and then shuffle them around until you are happy with them. For longer features, you need to plan ahead to make sure that the tone and balance of the piece are right as well as the structure and grammar.

Make a rough plan for yourself right at the beginning; this enables you to identify the broad areas you are planning to cover, and so makes it much easier to do the feature once you sit down at your desk. For example, if you interview a schoolboy squash player who has made it into the England squad, how would you put a piece together in 2000 words?

First, there's the opening paragraph – the introduction that you hope will be so 'grabbing' and exciting that it will hold people's attention and encourage them to read your piece. In the example, the angle is that a very young boy has been selected to play in a tough, well-established squad. You may therefore have chosen to interview him at school in the play-ground, or at home with his parents, to give you an angle for your story. This is where 'thinking like a magazine journalist' is really important. You need to consider the importance of marrying words and pictures, just as a television journalist must. The images in a magazine are vitally important, and editors know that if after you have written your piece they have to scratch around looking for pictures with which to illustrate it, it will never come across as a complete package.

If you aim to talk to your subject in suitable surroundings – like the school playground if the story is about a young boy making it to the top, or at a city law firm if the story is about a successful solicitor playing darts – then you have some background material that can be woven into the feature to create tensions and provide colour and life to the character you are portraying.

I once did an interview with a famous athlete who is renowned for being desperately difficult to get hold of. I eventually offered to do the interview in the car on the way to his next meeting so he could fit me in. It was the best decision I could have taken. Getting the point across about just how busy the man is could not have been done more logically, and I was able to refer to the journey during the piece, talking about his gear changes and contrasting his driving with his running for maximum effect.

Structure

Having a theme running through a piece helps to give structure and a framework to an interview. It is extremely difficult to write a themed piece without planning properly.

With a good framework finding the 'hook' for the piece should be relatively easy and unforced. In our sample case, this might be a look at the young boy in his natural surroundings – playing marbles, chatting to his friends, in short behaving like a 'normal' schoolboy. After the intro, you then need to open out the feature and expand on the story. So, your intro may be as follows:

> "Watching James Bush with his friends in the school playground, it's difficult to imagine him travelling the globe to represent England and competing with the best international squash players. But the 15-year-old from Essex has shattered all the records and last week became the youngest ever squash player in a world tournament."

Your follow-up paragraphs would then explain – with colourful anecdotes about how he got where he is – things like the hard work he had to put in and what it was like for him when he heard he had been selected.

Your feature needs to be given depth and credibility with quotes and references to other people. What did his Mum think? Ask him, by all means, but how about going to see her? Talk to his friends in the play-ground about their reactions; talk to teachers (maybe they're a bit worried that his school work will suffer?) and to his coach – is he pushing the boy too fast too soon? A doctor could be contacted to find out whether it's safe for a boy of this age to be playing at such a very high standard. Then there are the other players in the team – what do they think about playing with a boy? Will they end up looking after him all the time?

You might also think about including some vital statistics for a panel in the feature. For example, find out how many rackets he gets through in a year, how fast he hits the ball and who his favourite player is.

When you wrap up the story it's always nice to come back to the original theme of the feature. In this example, if you became concerned through the interview that the boy was doing too much too young, you may finish off the interview by saying that as you stood up to walk away and he walked alone back into the deserted school building, you realised that this boy's life had changed forever – and you couldn't help but think that in many ways it was a sad thing. It pulls all the strings together nicely if you can package up all the various views and thoughts of people connected to the story and then come back to the principle character at the end.

Style hints

In addition to having a clear idea about how to structure a story, it is useful to get a working grasp of the grammatical tools that will help you as you proceed with your feature.

No-one is suggesting that you should write your features like a school essay. However, just reminding yourself occasionally of the many ways in which you can write your features will help you to keep descriptions and observations fresh and interesting in your copy. Here are seven of the key tools that you should be aware of when it comes to feature writing.

Clichés

Try to avoid gratuitous *clichés* which add little to your writing. Clichés are phrases which started out as a brilliant way in which to describe something, and end up being used so often that their meaning is almost lost. If you use a desperately over-worked cliché it will add nothing to your work because people will think of the cliché and not what it represents in the context of your piece. Football reporting used to have a dreadful reputation for being built on a series of clichés, but clever journalism has served to wreck that reputation.

Euphemisms

These are used far too extensively in sport, but under the right circumstances they can be witty, descriptive and helpful. They are words or phrases which are used to replace words or phrases that could cause offence – for example, saying that someone has 'passed away' instead of saying that they have died. In sport, you may say that a manager has been asked to 'clear his desk', or a footballer has 'hung up his boots' instead of saying that the manager has been sacked and the footballer has retired.

Idioms

Sport has its own collection of unique idioms and all readers of sports publications will be familiar with them! They are phrases that sum up a situation without necessarily making sense in the context in which they are applied. For example, if an ice skater hears that her father is ill, and then her coach drops her from the team the next day, you might say that he was 'rubbing salt in the wound'. Footballers who miss the goal but hit the goal post are said the have 'rattled the woodwork'. And if a team plays brilliantly in one half and poorly in the other, journalists will say that it was 'a game of two halves'.

Metaphor

These are a lovely way of creating an image of the scene in the minds of your readers. Using a good metaphor can save hundreds of words of description. Essentially, a metaphor helps the readers to picture an event: for example, 'a crazy beast, throwing punches at his opponent'.

A metaphor is the process of using a colourful example to describe an event you are witnessing without using 'like' or 'as' – in the above example you have said that the boxer IS a crazy beast for literary reasons. A *simile* has a subtle difference to a metaphor.

Simile

The name says it all: when you use a simile you are saying that two things are *similar* to one another. This is done by using comparative words – *like* or *as*.

- He fought furiously, *like* a crazy beast.
- He fought furiously, *as though* he were a crazy beast.

Similes are another great way of getting your message across crisply and elegantly. You are using words to create a picture in the readers' minds. The best way to encourage readers to create a picture is to get them thinking about something they know well in the context of your piece.

Syntax

This is the process of putting together the words in a sentence in the correct order, so that the meaning is clear. If you say in a match report, "After falling from the beam and breaking an ankle, the physio has recommended that Olga Korbut should retire from the Olympic Games", it may be clear what is meant from the *sense* of the sentence, but it is the physio who has the broken ankle and not the leading Russian gymnast. The *syntax* is wrong.

In this example, it would not be the end of the world if the sentence made it into print, because the meaning is clear. However, there will be times when confusion is caused if busy sentences with several clauses are not syntactically correct.

The most common cause of problems in this area is cluttering a sentence with clauses so that the subject and the object of the sentence become confused. Unless you feel confident in your own ability and grammatical knowledge, you will lose nothing by just keeping sentences short and simple.

Tautology

This is the process of fanatically emphasising the brilliance of play. Sports writers indulge in the noble art of tautology on a daily basis. In fact it is wrong. It is a waste of words and usually unnecessary.

Tautology uses different words to say the same thing, for example: 'Jonah Lomu is a big giant of a man.' Is it possible to have a small giant? Of course not. The use of the word 'big' is entirely unnecessary. Often, when world records are broken or tries, goals or baskets are scored, tautology is used. A goal can be 'a wonderful, fantastic, top-class piece of action', and a near-miss can be 'so close, almost there, just missed'. Using the right word in the first place, or using a clever simile or metaphor can save you all this!

Sports Magazine Style Sheet – a Sample

ABBREVIATIONS   Unless an abbreviation is so familiar that it is used more often than the full form (eg, BBC, EU), write the words in full on first appearance: thus the Rugby Football Union (not RFU) on first mention. Most organisations should be preceded by 'the' (the FA). Spell out Professor, Colonel, Lieutenant, etc. in full in first instance in feature. Abbreviated form can be used in captions.

ACCENTS   On words now accepted as English, use accents only when they make a crucial different to pronunciation: cliché, café. If you use accents, make sure you use them all: résumé. All accents to be used on French words, and umlauts on German ones. Leave the accents off Spanish and other foreign words.

ADDRESSES   Comma always before postcode. Always include county with the town. Use commas to separate town and county from name and rest of information, eg James Hanning, from Basildon in Essex, played for Bath.

ALL RIGHT   (**never** alright)

AMONG   (not amongst)

AMPERSANDS (&)   Use only when part of the name of a company.

APOSTROPHES   Use normal possessive end ('s) after singular words or names that end in s, eg boss's, James's. Use the ending s' on plurals that end in s: bosses', Barclays', '60s (**not** 60's). When subbing on Mac, make sure you use shift, alt +] for '; alt +] for '; shift, alt +[for "; alt + [for ".

ASSOCIATIONS
AAA – Amateur Athletics Association
BAGA – British Amateur Gymnastics Association

BLUE   (cap B) as in Oxford/Cambridge

BRACKETS   Try to avoid using brackets – use dashes instead. If a whole sentence is within brackets, put the full stop inside. Square brackets should be used when additional information is added to the original text by the editor/sub.

CAPITALS   Organisations must have capitals, but not people's titles unless when used with their name. Eg, President Clinton, but the president; the chairman of the RFU. Government departments take capitals, eg, Department of Trade. Also acts, the Health and Safety at Work Act. If mentioning the House of Commons, it can then be referred to as the House; the Bank of England can then be referred to as the Bank. Parliament, the Opposition, the Queen and God always upper case. Government is upper case when preceded by 'the'; a government department etc is lower case. Capital R for river when preceding the name, eg, River Thames.

CENTRED ON   (not around or in)

CENTURY   (lc – mid-19th century)

in the CIRCUMSTANCES (not under the circumstances)

COLLECTIVE NOUNS   There is no firm rule about the number of a verb governed by a singular collective noun. It is best to go by the sense, ie, whether the collective noun stands for a single entity. Eg, The council was elected in March; The Army is on a voluntary basis. Or for its constituents: The council are at sixes and sevens; the Army are above the average civilian height. A safe rule for number: The number is .... A number are.....
   A government, a party, a company (whether Tesco or Marks and Spencer) and a partnership (Owings & Merrill) are all 'it' and take singular verb. So does a country, even if its name looks plural, eg the United States, is helping. The United Nations is singular, so is politics and economics.

COMMAS   Do not put a comma before 'and' at the end of a sequence of items unless one item includes another, eg, its main exports were tobacco, asbestos, meat and copper. But its main exports were tobacco, asbestos, meat and hides, and copper.

COMPANIES   Call companies by the names they call themselves. Eg, Chesebrough-Pond's, Lloyds (the bank), Lloyd's (the insurance market).

COMPARE   'Compare with' when you draw attention to the different. 'Compare to' when you want to stress their similarity, eg, Shall I compare thee to a summer's day?

COMPRISE   Comprise means 'is composed of'. Eg, the group comprises seven people. **Never** comprises of.

CURRENCY   1p to 99p (not £0.99). £6 (not £6.00). £3.50 (not £3.50p). £5,000 to £6,000. £5m to £6.

DASHES   Full em-width dashes (alt and dash on Mac). Dash for hyphens.

DATES   Commas between date and year, eg July 5, 1993. Date always follows month. July 5–6 not July 5 & 6, 1980s, '60s, '70s, 20th century, 20th anniversary, 1991–92. Second World War, First World War (note upper case), never World War I or World War II. Post-war and pre-war should be hyphenated. In general give dates: last week or last month can cause confusion. If the date is not known, use 'recently'.

DESPATCH   (not dispatch)

DIFFERENT   from (not different to or different than)

ETC, IE.   Avoid using if possible. For etc, use 'and so on' instead.

FEWER/LESS   Fewer refers to number; less refers to quantity. Eg, there were fewer than seven people with less hair.

FIGURES   Never start a sentence with a figure. If possible, rewrite the sentence; otherwise write the number in words. Use figures for numerals from 10 upwards and for all numerals that include a decimal point or a fraction. Use words for numerals from one to nine except when referring to page numbers and in lists of numerals, eg deaths from this cause in the past three years were 14, 9 and 6. Fractions should be hyphenated, eg, two-thirds, five-eighths.

FIRST   (not firstly. Same with second, not secondly)

Five Nations Championship

GREAT BRITAIN = England, Scotland and Wales

UNITED KINGDOM = England, Scotland, Wales and Northern Ireland.

haka (Maori war chant)

HYPHENS   Use hyphens for fractions (one-third, two-fifths); most words with anti-, non- and neo- (non-payment, anti-fascist) although there are exceptions (anticlimax, nonstop); a sum followed by the word worth (£10-worth of goods); some titles (under-secretary, vice-chairman etc); to avoid ambiguities (a little-used car, a little used-car); adjectives formed from two or more words (balance-of-payments difficulties, value-added tax); separating identical letters (book-keeping, pre-eminent, re-entry); quarters of the compass (north-east, south-eastern); nouns from prepositional verbs (build-up, call-up, get-together).

INITIALS   Initials in people's names take points, eg Mr I.F. Stone. Do not use full stops in company names, eg W & G Waterstone.

ITALICS   For magazines, newspapers (only *The Economist* and *The Times* have *The* italicised, so the *Daily Telegraph*, the *Observer*), works of art, books, TV programmes and ships' names. Also, foreign words not commonly used (see dictionary) and names of organisations. Latin names for plants and animals, but only the first word has a capital (eg, *Arenicola marina*). Use italics for emphasis rather than capitals – He was the person of the moment. Do not use italics in titles or captions.

it's = it is, eg it's a fine day

its   is possessive, eg I saw its mate

LAST   The last issue of Rugby World implies its extinction. Use instead last month's issue. Also, past instead of last, eg over the past year or past week.

LEAGUES/Divisions   National Leagues One, Two, Three, Four, Five North and Five South – never Divisions. Cap L for Leagues.

LEARNT   (rather than learned, same with dreamt, leant and spelt)

LINE-OUT   (with hyphen)

MEASUREMENT   Yards is always written in full, eg the ball was 17 yards long. If several measurements, write the box measured 17 yards x 14 yards. Inches and feet are always abbreviated to 'in' (never ins) and 'ft' when followed by a number, eg the ball was 13in long. The same applies to kg, km, lb (never lbs), oz (never ozs), dr (for dram), g (for gram) and mph. If using ft and in, add equivalent in metres in brackets. Same with stones, lb and oz, add kg in brackets – He was 6ft (1.83m) tall and weighted 17st 2lb (108.9kg).

MIDDAY   (not mid-day)

NONE   usually takes a singular verb. So does 'neither A nor B' unless B is plural. Eg, neither the Dutchman nor the Danes have done it.

NO ONE   (never no-one)

NORTHERN/southern hemisphere (lc)

ONLY   Put as close as possible to words it qualifies. Eg, these animals mate only in June. To say they only mate in June implies that in June they do nothing else.

PER CENT   (not % except in tables or lists), but percentage

Pilkington   Cup/Shield

PRACTICE   (noun)/practise(verb): Eg, I need to practise my penalty kicks

POSITIONS   No10 (no space, no .), three-quarters, half-back, full-back, scrum-half, loose-head prop, tight-head prop (with hyphens).

PROGRAMME/PROGRAM   Program a computer or have a computer program, but in all other contexts the word is programme.

QUOTES   Use double inverted commas for quotes, except when a quote is within a quote, eg "He said to me: 'I dislike fish' and I agreed."

SEVENS   rugby (not 7's, 7s or seven's)

SHORT WORDS   Use shorter words that are easy to understand, eg about, rather than approximately; let, rather than permit; buy, rather than purchase; use, rather than utilise.

SPRINGBOK(S)

SWAP   (not swop)

TELEPHONE NUMBERS   Abbreviate telephone to 'tel' with the code always in brackets, eg tel (0900) 123456.

Test matches (cap T)

TITLES   When title is long, eg vice-chairman of the Rugby Football Union, put person's name before title. Eg, Ronald Reagan, vice-chairman of the Rugby etc – not vice-chairman of the Rugby Football Union Ronald Reagan. Where the title is short, the opposite applies.

TRADE NAMES   Always appear in upper case, eg Hoover, Thermos, Coke, Velcro.

TRANSVAAL

UNDER-15, Under-21 (cap U)

UNIVERSITY   (never abbreviated to U)

WEIGHTS   lb for pound weight both singular and plural, eg 6lb, oz for ounces singular and plural.

Interviewing

This is when you really start to feel like the journalist you always dreamt you would be! You set off, clutching your note-book, tape recorder and sample questions and off you go for your first interview. Meeting people and getting to know them, then turning what you have learnt about them into a lively accessible article, is what a great deal of journalism is all about. But how do you go about planning properly, doing the research that is necessary and asking all the right questions so that you get the piece you want?

Planning
Everyone's approach to interviewing varies, but what all good interviewers do is *plan properly in advance*.

We touched earlier on the idea that the structure and tone of an article can be improved if you set the interview in a context that can be developed as a theme throughout the feature. In sport, this may be at a training night, on the edge of a pitch where a player played his first game (if you want someone to come out with some reflective, nostalgia-type quotes), or even in a totally alien setting where they may give a little more of their personality away.

As soon as you start to think like this, you realise that the planning has to start really early. Before you can even set up the interview venue, you need to have a clear idea of what the person is like and where they will best respond to you. One of the best ways of doing research is through old cuttings – if you have been able to get a cuttings file together yourself, then you may have all the information you need; if not, the magazine you are planning to write for may have cuttings. Alternatively, you could visit the library or 'phone around the subject' to get a feel for what the person is like.

You may find that despite your best efforts, the interviewee refuses to talk to you anywhere other than in the club-house after training. It maybe because he's busy, in which case you can ask him all about his busy lifestyle and weave it into the piece. If he is just stubborn, is it his stubbornness that makes him a tough player? You don't have to act as an amateur psychologist and try to second-guess everyone's inner feelings and motivations, but there may be a line for your piece on the interviewee's reaction to your request.

As well as thinking clearly about the person you are going to interview and what sort of character they are, you also need to ask yourself at the beginning of the exercise exactly why you are doing the interview. What is the main purpose of it? Why do the magazine readers want to know about this person? Until you know what you're after from the piece, you can never set out to achieve it.

Making your approach

Once you have cleared up in your own mind why you are doing the interview and what sort of person you will be dealing with, you need to make your approach.

The beauty of most sportsmen and women is that they are actually quite sociable people and are usually really good fun. If they are amateurs they are quite down to earth and probably enjoy the attention, and if they are professional there will often be an onus on them to talk to the press and thus raise the profile of their club or sport.

The biggest problem can be getting hold of them in the first place, but if you have got good reliable contacts as we discussed in chapter one, then you should be able to pin down a contact number for the person you want to talk to. If you can't get hold of a personal number, you have several options. Does the magazine itself have a number that you could try? If that draws a blank, then the traditional way of getting hold of someone is to phone the club and explain to the press officer what you are trying to do. The press officer might give you a number straight off if he knows you, or he might put you in touch with an agent or manager. If he is unco-operative – as they sometimes can be – then the option left is to send a letter or fax through to the club, or turn up on a training night and approach your subject directly with your request.

It can sometimes be that a player is simply not getting your message, or is too busy to stop and talk. If you turn up and ask politely if he can spare half an hour some time soon, then you may find you get a favourable response from him. The key is to make sure that you are always polite. You may be dealing with a professional sportsman who has been interviewed hundreds of times, but you still have to take control of the situation and make sure that he is both happy with the way things are proceeding and confident enough in your abilities to grant you some time.

If you have ever been interviewed for a newspaper or magazine, you will know how nerve-wracking it can be. Even seasoned professionals know how much they can be stitched up by an up-and-coming journalist who wants to make a mark in the profession. Be cautious but confident and go through the correct channels before you start pursuing players by following them to the shops or turning up at their children's parents' day. If you think you're being held at arm's length by over-protective club officials, and if you really believe that if you could meet the interviewee to talk to him things would be OK, then turning up on training night, catching him in the bar after a match or getting hold of him in some other place that relates to the sport is more acceptable than ringing him up at 11.00 p.m. at night when he's at home with his family.

Planning the interview itself

If you have planned the whole project carefully, and know where you would like to talk to him, what other people you intend to talk to, and what the main thrust of the story is going to be, you then need to think carefully about the interview time itself. Consider what questions you need to ask in order to really understand the person, and in particular get the information about the story behind the sportsman.

There are a million different ways of doing this, but there are three very broad approaches. The first is to turn up with a strict list of questions that need answering and persist until they are answered – that way you will have all the foundation blocks you need in order to build the article when you get back. You will have no superfluous chatter to wade through on your tape; just information that is entirely relevant to the piece you want to create.

The problem with this approach is that you are actually creating a story before you get there. One of the most common mistakes in feature writing is not giving the interviewee any chance to actually tell you what he's like, how he feels or what's important to him. If you ask a list of questions that fit a tightly controlled brief, then you will get no real feeling for the man other than how he responds to set key questions. It may be that the real story is much more interesting than the one you came expecting!

The second approach is to do all your research into the person you are going to talk to, but then just to chat to him. Let the conversation run and see what he's like and how he interacts with you. The problem with this is that if you go without a set brief, you may miss the opportunity to probe deeper or really challenge him. He may then come across as being rather vacuous in print, and you don't get a good story.

The third option is the one to strive for if you can. Have a list of questions with you, but spend the first part of the interview chatting to the subject – getting him to like and trust you while you glean all sorts of information about his mannerisms and personality to colour the piece with. Then, move into your key questions. Make sure you only have a few really important ones rather than an enormous list,– and let the interviewee expand on his answers. Challenge him on his replies and get good, solid, in-depth answers to really important issues rather than asking him a million quick-fire questions. You can get all the information that you would normally get from quick-fire questions through your earlier chat with him.

Writing it up

If at all possible, write up your interview straight away. The more distant your meeting with him becomes, the less fresh and lively your copy will seem. The memories of the look on his face when he talked about losing the World Championships, or the delight he showed when you mentioned his new coach, will start to fade very quickly.

Even if you don't have a couple of hours in which to sit down and actually write up the piece, how about spending half an hour just jotting down anything that intrigued, interested or surprised you, a brief description of the scene, and your feeling about the interviewee immediately after the interview. At least you will then have some information to base a report on when you come to write the piece. Anything that amazed you when you talked to him – after all your research – is sure to amaze the readers too, so write it down before you forget.

The basic structure of features has been discussed earlier in this chapter. However, do remember to check with the editor what particular style the interview should be in. Do they want a traditional feature, something with a bit more of a 'lifestyle' theme (giving colour to the character rather than to the story), or do they want the piece in simple question-and-answer format? They will undoubtedly have told you as they commissioned you, but it is well worth checking with them one more time in case things have changed since you last spoke to them.

Once the interview is published, send a copy of the publication to the interviewee with a thank-you note if you can. If an agent or manager helped you get the interview, it would be polite – and useful in terms of cultivating your relationship with him – to send him a copy as well.

9 • TELEVISION

Why television?

Television remains the most alluring of all the media for would-be sports journalists. Its ability to bring words and pictures into the homes of everyone in the country within milliseconds of the action taking place makes the prospect of a career in it as attractive as ever.

Television is seen as being the ultimate in glamour, offering the chance to travel around following your chosen sport whilst instantly becoming famous and being paid phenomenal salaries. You can be at the forefront of communication by informing viewers about everything as it happens – from news of team selection or interviews to match reports beamed live into people's living rooms from anywhere in the world. The moving pictures, along with the ability to speed things up and slow things down, pause the action and show statistics and information from past events, makes television a fantastic medium for sports journalists. But there are some drawbacks; most notably the fact that you are judged by television producers for qualities other than just your writing skills. Suddenly the way you look, the way you dress, your mannerisms and your voice have as much bearing on your ability to succeed as your ability to write and deliver knowledgeable sports information.

So, you may be a brilliant, competent journalist with a real ability to perform well under pressure, but a former sports star or a younger, more attractive presenter may get the nod over you – there is nothing you can do about it.

ITV's Head of Rugby Coverage, Simon Moore, sums up the attributes you need to succeed in television.

"There are obviously different requirements for different areas of television sports journalism. For instance, it helps if a presenter looks good and has a pleasing personality – a commentator must have a voice that's easy on the ear, and so on. But if there's one thing that unites all those who work in TV sport, and indeed in any kind of television journalism, I believe it's the ability to marry words with pictures. It's no good writing the most sublime prose if it doesn't match your shots. It sounds very basic, but its a discipline that the very best sports journalists use every working day.

I think a good television journalist needs to always deal in pictures. The first question that he or she should ask when approaching a report, documentary or commentary is, 'What will we see?', because that's the key to everything else."

ne good news is that television is growing at an extraordinary rate, and there are more opportunities than ever to get involved. No longer is it the reserve of Oxbridge graduates who wear the right schoolties and whose father served in Africa with the Director General of the BBC! A multitude of satellite channels, each serving a different market, and all – to a greater or lesser extent – covering sport, have shot up in the last decade.

Understanding the roles

There is a hierarchy that exists in television production. The executive producer is in charge of policy decision-making, advanced fixing and delegating. The producer is directly below him, usually assigned to a specific programme. He will be responsible for filling the air-time with features that viewers will be interested in. Below the producer is the assistant producer; his work is with a particular slot on the programme. With every outside broadcast, every story fed into a programme and every highlights package, there will be an assistant producer with responsibility for that section. He will manage the team of reporter, cameraman and sound engineer on the shoot.

The assistant producers (sometimes known as production assistants) have regular meetings with the producer of a show to brainstorm ideas and discuss good practices, in the same way that an editorial team would meet regularly with the editor to discuss ideas and concepts.

The director (not all programmes have them, and very few sports programmes do) would decide which pictures go on air, with the production assistant working with him to ensure that the message is brought across clearly. Directors are found in live television broadcasts when there are decisions constantly to be made about angles, interweaving interviews and video tapes, and sounds.

On the editorial side there are also several roles. There is the freelance journalist who offers suggestions and contributes news stories (as with radio). These tend to be working on local papers where they pick up stories that they then feed through to television stations. They are known as *stringers*, and they get paid for any suggestions that are followed up. They are encouraged to phone in with all the ideas they have, and provide much of the basic news. A good, reliable network of stringers is cultivated by all sports news editors – they tend to have good contacts in clubs and with the players and athletes, so they can be relied upon to provide many leading stories.

There is also a team in the newsroom that is dedicated solely to sport. The size of the team depends on the area being covered and the budgets available for sport.

Television sports news teams can rely fairly heavily on their own out-stations for stories. Material that is originated locally can be fed into live network sports bulletins, or fed non-live into later shows. This means that the humble stringer who is providing a few leads to an over-worked producer at a small local station may find his story appearing as a leading national sports story later in the day.

This sharing of information is a two-way process. Regional broadcasting teams can access local stories arising from national stories at the London centre. The large networks have become much better at sharing resources recently, so that if there is a local angle to a big national story, the local stations can access video tape from the national film crews with which to illustrate their stories.

This happens with both BBC and Independent Television Companies. The third force in television sport is Sky, which is slowly moving itself into a leading position in terms of sports coverage. Its signing up of the big sports for exclusive coverage rights is making it a very attractive work-place for sports journalists. At the moment it makes use of agencies for much of its output, and feeds this into an anchor sports presenter who holds the shows together. Sky is increasingly employing its own reporters and camera crews as it becomes more and more established in the market-place.

Types of on-screen reporting

One of the most difficult pieces for a novice reporter is the *piece to camera*. It feels completely unnatural to be standing facing a cameraman in a bizarre location, while a fascinated crowd gathers round you. Remembering the words can be extremely difficult, and every time you make a mistake you feel more embarrassed about the whole affair. But the piece to camera is favoured by producers because it is easy to film, you can prove that the reporter is there on the spot, and it can be produced as a contained report which makes editing easier. Reporters therefore have to learn to do them in as professional a way as possible.

The best way to cope with pieces to camera in the early days is to keep the length of narrative down to the maximum that you can remember without difficulty (usually around 10–15 seconds). The alternative is to make the opening paragraph word-perfect, then read or refer to the rest from a clipboard. If you are really stuck, it is possible to do pieces to camera in several takes and stick them together with some action sliced in; or with the reporter in a slightly different place in the second piece so as to avoid a 'jump' in the edit. However, this creates a lot more work for everyone, so is usually avoided if it's at all possible to do it in one take.

Studio spots

A studio spot is when a piece is read out by someone other than the main newscaster or presenter (for example, the football correspondent reporting during a sports round-up).

Where sport is concerned, it is often the sports reporter himself who is the studio spot because most sports bulletins lie at the end of a news programme. They can be easier than doing pieces to camera on location because of the use of auto-cue and the fact that scripts can be prepared well, and read out from the relative comfort of a desk instead of on the edge of a football pitch. But they have difficulties all of their own because of the lights and noise in a studio, having to react with other reporters on screen, and coping with the ear-piece.

The interview

Many sports slots rely on interviews to extract information. Even if there is an investigative story to be told it will usually be played out through interviewing key people in the story, so sports journalists have to be able to master the ability to interview for television.

There is a balance to be struck in interviewing between badgering and hassling an athlete for information – which immediately sets him and the audience against you – and being too soft so that he doesn't answer pertinent questions. There are also various types of interviews, based largely on where they are conducted.

- The *set piece* interview is conducted at the interviewee's choice of location – his home, his club, or a hotel or restaurant that he suggests.
- The second method is the *vox pop* interview, where members of the public are talked to at random and asked for their opinion. The views canvassed in this way are valuable to the extent that they represent public opinion on a sports story rather than the players' or the coach's feelings.
- The *door-stepper* interview is the hardest to do because the interviewee often does not want to talk to you. In sport there are not too many of these to do; but every time there is a drugs scandal or a player caught in bed with a barmaid, someone somewhere has to get the story.
- *Eye-witness* or on-the-spot interviews gather facts immediately after something has happened. If the Football Association is drawing up new guidelines, there will be journalists waiting outside Lancaster Gate to talk to them the minute the meeting finishes.

The final interview method is the news conference, where journalists gather round to interview a player after a match or to hear an announce-ment or big new sponsor signing. The location and the line of questioning are largely out of the hands of the individual, but the television journalist must make sure that he asks a couple of questions in order to have the interviewee facing the camera with his answers.

It can be extremely difficult to interview for television, because you have to come straight to the point all the time. There is no room for chatting casually to the subject first, like there is in newspaper reporting; nor for getting to know them over lunch. You have to ask pertinent questions almost straight away, and be prepared to repeat them several times to get a worthy answer for broadcast.

The television journalist also has to cope well with the answers he gets, and can't spend much thinking time on camera. It can be tough, but a good television interviewer will always find work.

Can you just write – or do you have to broadcast?

Not every journalist automatically appears in front of the cameras. A great deal of journalistic expertise goes into producing ideas for features and scripts. It rather depends on the organisation that you work for as to whether or not you will appear in front of the camera.

Satellite station Channel One has revolutionised television by having their journalists carry portable cameras. They research their story, then set the camera up and talk to the lens to record their piece. They can then take it back to the studio where it is edited for transmission. However, some stations still make massive distinctions between journalists who perform and journalists who edit and write.

If you are interested in working for television as a sports writer, you are likely to need experience in working on the sports desk of a newspaper. You will certainly need proof that you can write well, and you will need to have an understanding of the differences between writing for readers and writing for viewers.

Unlike writing for newspapers or magazines, the style-sheet approach cannot be applied rigidly on television. Producers accept that they cannot have complete control over every single word spoken by every single contributor – whether they are reporters, interviewees or participants. In any two-minute news package there will be a number of influences which cannot be tightly controlled individually, like they are by a newspaper reporter, but which must meet certain editorial and production standards when put together.

For example, a sports news feature may include: a few words from the anchor presenter into an opening sequence with out-of-vision words; an interview; more pictures and commentary; another word or two from the interviewee; and a piece to camera from the reporter to wrap it all up. All these elements need to be melded into one to convey the facts in a concise, interesting way that every viewer can easily understand. This is very difficult in television, which doesn't benefit from knowing as much about the customer as other forms of media. For example, newspaper buyers will choose between the *Daily Mirror* or the *Daily Telegraph* because they prefer either the bright and breezy style of the *Mirror* or the more sober and 'heavier' approach of the *Telegraph*. The differences between ITV, BBC and Sky are nowhere near as marked.

Writing for television involves striking the balance between being condescending and being highbrow. You have to write for *speech*, so language should be conversational without being intellectually insulting. It used to be the case that television writers would read out scripts for typists to input, rather than scribble them down – this gave them a clear idea of how the words sounded. The computer has done away with this testing method, so journalists now resort to reading their scripts to one another to hear what they sound like.

How to get involved

Despite the fact that television is growing at an astonishing rate, with satellite stations being set up everywhere and offering more and more chances for journalists to get involved, there have been so many cut-backs and rationalisations in mainstream television that it is still as difficult and competitive as ever to break in.

Full-time jobs in television are extremely hard to come by without considerable experience. Freelance work and short-term engagements – i.e. contracts of 364 days or fewer – are fast becoming the norm. Added to this is the fact that there are hundreds of people with a great deal of experience applying for every job out there because of redundancies, so that getting in at entry level without experience is very difficult.

It does help if you know someone, simply because it will be assumed that you have a greater understanding of the demands of television if you can boast a family member or friend who is involved in the industry. It's much easier for a television company to justify taking risks with a new writer or presenter if that person has at least some understanding of the industry. There is also the simple fact that you are more likely to know the right people to contact to find out if there are any vacancies around in the first place.

Ultimately, however, whether you get a break because your brother-in-law is head of sport, or because you continually and relentlessly send in letters and ideas to the television companies, does not matter. It might make for an easy break, but that is all – because if there's one thing you can be sure of, it's that the work of a writer and broadcaster is scrutinised and analysed by so many people that those writers who are not up to it will simply not remain involved. There's no opportunity for bad or unpopular writers to keep their jobs in such a high-profile industry.

Getting involved

The best way of getting into television sports journalism is the same as getting involved in any other areas of sports journalism – pure, unadulterated effort. You need to do plenty of ground-work to get a foot in the door, and it will help if you have at least some experience – for example, if you have worked in hospital broadcasting, or indeed any area of the voluntary sector, or have some experience of professional writing (don't send in school essays or projects – these won't impress anyone).

You need to emphasise early on in your application that you understand the importance of team-work in television. It's not like writing for the print media where you are essentially working on your own during the writing stage. Television really is all about working pictures and words together through the use of the latest technology.

If you think you'd like to work in television you have several options. You can, of course, apply for jobs as they come up. They are advertised in the *Guardian* on Mondays, and in *The Stage* and the *UK Press Gazette* as well as in a host of other publications. It's well worth contacting any station you are interested in working for to enquire about vacancies and when they are likely to come up. However, the trouble with just replying to a job advertisement is that it's very unlikely that you will stand a chance of getting the job if you have no television experience.

Getting some sort of experience is vital. First, you can make sure that you really do understand the industry and are sure that you want to work in it. Second, it gives you some credibility when you come to put your CV together. It also helps you to meet other people in the industry and start that vital process known as making contacts or *networking*.

Courses

Many of the broadcasting networks – the BBC in particular – run courses designed to introduce candidates to all areas of television. You cannot specialise in sport on these courses, just as you cannot specialise in sport on newspaper courses; but if you have an interest in sport, and make yourself as knowledgeable as possible while you are on a television course, you may find an opening to specialise once the course is finished. However, by far the most common way to get involved in covering sport on television is to write to your local television station with any ideas you might have for features and why you think you would be suitably qualified to work for them.

Writing off to television producers

If there is a particular specialist sports programme that you are keen to work for, send off a letter directly to the producer of that programme. Don't rely on books for information about who the producer is – the person may have changed. It's much better to actually ring up and find out who the current producer is.

I wrote to Rugby Special totally off the cuff one evening, because I was desperate to have a go at working in television and I saw a million opportunities for me to get involved in that programme. Since they had the regular highlights section of the programme all sewn up, I decided that coming up with alternative ideas would be much better. If you are going to do this, you have to 'sell' your idea to the television producers as well as selling yourself as the ideal person to present the new feature idea – despite the fact that you have absolutely no broadcasting experience! The way to sell an idea to a producer is to convince him that there is an untapped market out there for the sort of feature that you are suggesting – but never criticise his programme unfairly in the process. Say that you're a fan of the programme and wondered whether they had ever thought about incorporating a youth section, a behind-the-scenes section or a fitness section or, alternatively, whether they had thought about doing an interview with ...

You then need to extol your own virtues, and explain why you think you're the perfect person to do the interview or feature. Most specialist sport programmes, like Ski Sunday or Rugby Special, are always on the look-out for new blood to inject some life into the programmes.

You will find it difficult to convince producers that you are the best person for the job if you have absolutely no television experience. If your lack of experience is continually preventing you from *gaining* experience, so that you are finding yourself caught in a vicious circle, you may opt to write to a producer and ask him whether he could possibly spare the time to meet you for a few minutes to discuss how you might get involved in television. A producer may be able to tell you what steps you should take to prepare yourself, or to let you have a list of courses that you could attend; or he may advise you to keep coming up with ideas until one hits the mark.

Alternatively, do what newspaper journalists do to get a portfolio together – offer to broadcast for nothing. Television presenter Carol Smile said:

> "When I was keen to break in to television I wrote to every production company and video company in Glasgow, saying that whatever they were doing I would present it for nothing. So I managed to get a few clips together of charity work and short promos to take into interviews with me."

Once you have a video example of your competence, at least the producer will have a feel for how you come over on screen as well as on paper and in the flesh.

Finding a direction

The lovely thing about having a clear direction is that when you do get a break on your ideal programme, you know you're working towards exactly where you want to be, without compromising. If you are just battling away trying to get any sort of break, this will never be the case.

However, you can't write off to the programme that you would most like to work for if you don't know what it is! You need to have *direction*, both in terms of the sort of programme you would like to work for (live, documentaries or highlight programmes) and of which sport you would like to specialise in.

The alternative to targeting a specialist sports programme is to contact local television stations with suggestions for features. You could write in with ideas about events coming up locally, if you think you know the area well; or just write in and express your interest saying that you would like to get involved in any way. If you are an expert in a particular sport you may be useful to them at some stage in the future. The other place you could try contacting with sports feature ideas are non-sports programmes that may entertain the idea of a sports slot in the future.

General television

Some daytime television programmes like Breakfast TV, mid-morning chat-shows and afternoon education programmes may consider having a sports slot if you can convince them that there is a real need for one. For example, you may suggest to daytime TV producers that they have a series which looks at different sports, discusses the health and fitness benefits of them, and uses sports as places for people to get out and meet people.

Alternatively, you might suggest to children's shows like *Newsround* that they have a regular sports up-date. It's worth a try – at least it gets your name about!

Points to remember about writing off 'on spec'

- Always type out your covering letter. Keep it short and snappy; make sure you include details of where you can be contacted, and all recent and *relevant* experience.

- It's useful to include a CV if you have lots of relevant experience. However, resist the urge to send a blanket CV off to everyone. If you have a computer and can store a blanket CV on one side of A4, you can go into the file and make any amendments so that the CV is tailor-made for the particular job you're applying for.

- If you're after a job which may lead to on-screen work, it's well worth enclosing a photograph, even if it's just a passport-sized one

- If you have any evidence of your experiences or abilities in front of the camera, make sure you enclose it (obviously, only if it shows you in a reasonable light!). The biggest problem that a producer will have when confronted with letters from would-be television presenters (and they do get a lot) is that they have no idea how the candidates will actually cope once the cameras start rolling. If you've done lots of television work don't enclose several tapes – enclose the best one, and mention the other television experience in the CV or covering letter. The tape you send should be a copy (if you really need it back enclose a stamped addressed envelope, but even then you can't guarantee that they will return it). Make sure you mark your tape clearly with your name and address because producers receive dozens of tapes.

- It's worth enclosing a couple of your best cuttings (make sure they are by-lined).

- Have referees listed at the bottom of your CV.

- Check and double-check your letter before sending it. If they spot mistakes at this stage it will reflect very badly on you.

Attending an interview

If your letter to the producer is successful and he decides he would like to see you to talk through your ideas, you have done extremely well. Be careful not to miss the opportunity to really seize hold of the advantage and get your foot firmly in the door.

That is not to say that you should be overly pushy, but make sure that every area of your presentation is spot on, and that you have done all your homework before arriving.

Obviously, it goes without saying that you should arrive punctually and dress appropriately. How you dress depends very much on the sort of work you hope to be doing. In sport, the dress codes are usually much less rigid than in news, but make sure you look smart, authoritative and credible. Also, make sure that you have a list of questions to ask – not just because it looks more impressive, but also because you genuinely should use the opportunity to find out all you can and raise all the queries you have.

It would also be useful if you offered ideas for stories; this shows that you have thought through the programme and have a full grasp of its aims. There is even the outside chance that he will really like one of your ideas, and decide to commission a piece!

Have you got what it takes?

It can be very difficult to tell whether you will make a good broadcaster if you've never tried it, and it can be extremely difficult to push yourself to a producer if you are unsure about whether you really have the skills it takes to succeed. Try reading through the following list to see which of the characteristics apply to you. They were all highlighted by a team of sports producers as being essential in a television sports journalist. The producers added that they would expect a would-be broadcaster to be able to *prove* they had each of these skills when sending in their preliminary letter and enclosures (CV, cuttings, tape).

- An ability to communicate well and professionally
- Good knowledge and understanding of sport
- A perfectionist who will work hard to do whatever has to be done to get the job done
- Experience that is directly relevant
- Initiative
- Flair – the ability to think laterally
- Genuine interest in television and sport
- Good general knowledge (news stories very often impact upon sports stories)
- An enquiring mind
- Originality and creativity
- Sense of humour

- Solid grounding in journalism skills
- A team player
- Great ideas
- Eager to try anything
- Persistence. If producers see you as persistent in terms of getting a job, they know you would be persistent when it comes to getting stories.

Direct training opportunities

Most forms of apprenticeships have gone by the board in television, but there are a few opportunities to get on to a *direct entry training course*. These are offered annually by employers, but it remains extremely difficult to get a place. The courses combine formal instruction with work placements in the various departments, so that the entrants can see how television works and establish fairly early on which of the areas they are interested in developing a career in.

There is no guarantee of work after being on a direct training course. Obviously, though, employers are more likely to give jobs to those candidates who have a knowledge of the industry through training courses; and obviously too, the fact that the television company has invested financially in your training means that they are infinitely more likely to look on your application favourably. There is also the fact that you are more likely to hear about job opportunities arising if you are already working in the company.

As television companies have cut back on staff, so the training opportunities have disappeared. This is to save money, and also because there is no point in companies running excellent training programmes if there are no jobs available to go to afterwards. The most prestigious of the training courses still run is the BBC's News Trainee Scheme. This has between 40 and 60 recruits a year depending on the calibre of the applications and, more likely, on the likelihood of job opportunities afterwards. ITV only has around 12 places on offer.

There is no opportunity to specialise in sport on these courses, but they give you an excellent all-round grounding in television, allowing you to specialise later on. If you apply for one of these places and make it to the interview stage, you have done extremely well. Be aware that the interview panel will be extremely tough on you as they work to establish who the few places should be awarded to. If you turn up for an interview without a thorough knowledge of the station's output, as well as some thoughts of your own as to what sort of programmes should be developed and why, you will find yourself coming unstuck under cross-examination. Your dress sense, your voice, your confidence and your enthusiasm will all be under the microscope. Many stations also run tests of general knowledge and analyse news sense by asking candidates to put a news bulletin in order.

If you do not get through the interview stage, do not be put off – there are very few places, and you did exceptionally well to make it that far.

However, you must make the most of the opportunity by contacting the interview panel and asking them what qualities they were looking for and where you went wrong. They should be prepared to give you some constructive feedback which can only help you in the future.

For details of other courses, contact the National Council for the Training of Broadcast Journalists, or consider looking at National Vocational Qualifications which have been developed over the last few years in order to define acceptable standards of competence for all areas in which assessment is necessary. Even sports coaching qualifications are ranked, and so can be compared to one another through the NVQ system. The qualifications are based on the ability of an individual to complete a series of tasks (known as *competencies*) in the work-place. There are several levels of NVQ; the lowest measures the most basic of skills, while the highest level (at the time of writing this is level five) measures the most complex of skills. The idea is that if you are awarded NVQ level five in television or level five in engineering your competence is about the same, so that senior managers can move within the industry more readily.

Overall management of NVQs for broadcasting, film and video is the responsibility of Skillset. This company is continually looking at and monitoring the needs of all who work in the industry.

There are two other points of entry into television journalism. The first is the regional press (the BBC say that most of their people have come through this route because it means they have experience of writing and understand sports news values on a day-to-day basis). The second is to try to get a job as a sports assistant and look for internal promotion. Sports assistants are like researchers – they supply information to producers. Unfortunately, there are very few sports assistant jobs, and once you get one there is no guarantee that you will be able to move on from it easily.

Life on screen

If your sports journalism dream is to appear on screen, then there are several areas you will be judged on, in addition to your ability to string words together and your knowledge of sport.

Details like speech, mannerisms and how you look and dress will become important. It's not just vanity that prompts presenters to look their best on the screen. It can be very distracting if a reporter has a twitch, cannot keep his hands still or is wearing an overly bright tie.

The adage that a picture is worth a thousand words is very true. No matter how world-shattering the information you are delivering is, if your clothing or mannerisms are distracting then it will be these that the viewer watches instead of listening to the words.

Mannerisms

All presenters have their own personal way of delivering information. It would be impossible to compare Dickie Davies, Sue Barker and Des Lynam

– but their personal style does not interfere with the delivery of the words. An eye movement or a nod of the head to emphasise a point is perfectly acceptable, but signs of stage fright like biting the lip, fiddling with things or constantly looking down at notes can be very off-putting.

It is usually felt that time will solve most of these problems, because so many of them are brought on with fear that dissolves with practice. However, if you feel that your appearance in front of the camera and your tendency to magnify normal movements under pressure, will lead to problems, then the only way to deal with them is to watch and learn. Video yourself and watch yourself carefully to see if you have any unusual mannerisms that you can work on sorting out. Take one thing at a time, and really concentrate on it next time you are filmed. Also, watch other presenters and see how they cope under pressure. The thing you must avoid doing at all costs, is to worry so much about a particular mannerism that it gets worse because you're piling the stress on!

Speech

The most important thing to remember about speech is not to attempt to remove all traces of accent, or adopt a home counties lilt overnight, but to work on delivering lines clearly and at an even pace.

Received pronunciation from the BBC used to come in the form of everyone sounding like middle-class southerners. The reason for this was because their accent was deemed more acceptable and easier to understand. Nowadays, the latter still applies; but it doesn't matter where you are from. If you can be clearly understood, and are talking at an even pace, your accent is irrelevant.

If you find it difficult to read out from scripts, make sure that it is not just you at fault! Bad writing causes problems as much as bad presentation. If you find you are stopping short, running out of breath or adding imaginary full-stops into sentences, it may be because the sentences are too long.

If you genuinely believe that you have difficulty with your speech, it may be your breathing that is causing problems and forcing you to gabble through to the end of the script before you take a breath. Practise reading with a tape recorder and listen to see where and when you make mistakes to see if a pattern emerges.

Dress

There is no hard and fast rule about what you should wear on camera; it rather depends on the nature of the programme you are working on. There are however certain guidelines that are worth adhering to.

- Striped and checked clothing can cause the picture to 'strobe' (like visual hiccups across the screen). It often happens with the ties of male newsreaders, and it is very distracting.

- Black and white should be avoided if possible because vision mixers use them to gauge contrast, and it makes their job a little harder.
- The other colour which has been known to cause trouble is blue. It can create the impression of a 'hole' through which studio backgrounds dramatically appear!

If you are in any doubt, always check with the producers before you start. Whatever you do, avoid anything distracting – dangling earrings and beads are a definite 'no-no', as are badges that can hardly be made out, because most viewers will be ignoring what you say while they watch your earrings swaying or try to make out what's on your lapel badge.

10 • RADIO

An odd concept?

Writing about sport for radio is an odd concept because sport is so visual. However, in a world where people are increasingly busy, and have less time to sit in front of the television, radio provides a very real way of keeping in touch with sport while on the move. Suddenly, you can access up-to-the-minute information about football results or the latest score in the cricket while you are sitting in the garden, in the car or on the train.

Radio's real beauty is its spontaneity, but in order to deliver this the presenter needs to be extremely disciplined and a real perfectionist. Radio 5's leading sports presenter, John Inverdale, says:

"Whilst spelling obviously isn't as important for a radio journalist as for those in the print world, an attention to detail is.

The good radio journalist has a genuine interest in the people he or she is talking to, which then comes over in the delivery of the piece and the intonation in the voice. Having a good voice is helpful, but not essential... having an interesting voice is more important.

The great broadcasters have a wide-ranging vocabulary, so that when live on air, the 'mot juste' is on their lips within milliseconds. Hear a poor broadcaster, and you realise how often they repeat the same words or phrases. Being widely read is far more important in the radio world as a consequence.

The crucial elements in the radio world that can distinguish it from other forms of the media is its immediacy, flexibility, spontaneity and simplicity. If you are spontaneous, flexible and above all else simple, you'll go far."

On the move

The arrival of personal stereos has made radio an even more important medium. It now allows listeners to enjoy radio broadcasts while moving around. During Wimbledon, people can be spotted enjoying every ball of the final as they do their shopping or take the dogs for a walk. This really does make a radio a key area, and a medium of communication which will be with us for a long time.

Radio monitors suggest that most members of the adult population listen to the radio at least once a day, so it is still an extremely wide audience. All the national and regional radio stations run news bulletins that contain sports information, many of them with a separate, dedicated sports presenter, and certainly with researchers and reporters on the look-out for the top sports stories of the day.

Another reason for radio's increasing importance is the arrival of Sky TV, which is forcing sport out of the public television domain. The main way now in which people without access to satellite television can 'witness' sport live is on radio. For writers, the great thing about radio is that unlike television, where the pictures can help to tell the story, radio is totally dominated by words. Even newspapers have some visual impact – with pictures, diagrams, charts, headlines and pull-out quotes – but on radio, the strength of the broadcast lives or dies by the ability to communicate effectively with words and sounds.

Radio has been around in Britain for over 75 years, and the quality and quantity of its sport content has progressed enormously over that time. Stations like Radio 5 exist to fulfil the demand for sports information on the radio in an era when so much of the population spends so much time on the road.

So in fact, far from being an odd concept, there is a very real and fast-growing market-place for sports journalists in radio. The role of the word-smith is absolutely vital – so it is an area which should not be ignored.

Background

Like those in television, and to a certain extent those in print journalism, radio journalists fall into two categories. There are those who plan and produce programmes; and there are those who actually fill the air-time (in newspapers, you might compare this to the journalists that fill the paper and the sports editor, sub-editors and designers who plan and produce the pages). The planners and producers tend to hold staff jobs, whereas many of the artists are freelance or on short-term contracts. Of course, there are full-time jobs to be had in radio as a broadcaster, but this distinction does still occur, and you may find that getting a full-time job is extremely difficult.

If you are really interested in radio, you are better off getting involved in any way you can – even if it is through a freelance opening rather than a full-time job. When you are on the inside, it will be much easier to wriggle your way into a full-time appointment by proving yourself to the people that matter, rather than waiting on the outside for an opportunity to come up. The production staff on radio will tend to be full-time (although again, this is not always the case – there are producers who free-lance, and there are those on short-term contracts). The producer's job is to have a full understanding of what the listeners require, and to fill the station's air-time with sports stories and news that the public will enjoy.

Have you got the necessary skills?

How do you know whether you have what it takes to be a top-notch sports radio journalist? The next section of this chapter will look at the writing skills you will need, and what the differences are between writing for radio and writing for print. However, the most obvious question to ask yourself in the first instance is: do you have a voice that's clearly understood? It doesn't make any difference whether you have an accent or not – there's no need to find yourself elocution lessons or perfect your vowel pronunciation – but the most important thing is that your voice is easy to listen to and easy to understand.

The only way to find this out is to try listening to yourself on a tape recorder. If you have an answerphone at home, you will know how odd your voice can sound when it's taped. The reason for this is that you hear the sounds differently when you are speaking yourself. You must get used to hearing and analysing the voice that listeners will hear when they tune into the radio station.

Presenting your words

Radio producers are quite scathing about sports journalists who make their name in print, then attempt the move into broadcasting. The main reason is that there is a big difference between the way that print journalists write their words out, and the way broadcasters write for radio. One of the key ways in which newspapers differ from radio is that you have to *present* the words – or, if you are just writing and not broadcasting, you have to write the words so they are fit to be broadcast (or 'performed') by the presenter and not read out in a monotone. A pure radio journalist will write a script suitable for radio rather than write a piece and read it out on radio. There is a subtle, but very key, difference.

The way in which the words are presented is as important as the words themselves; they need to be handed to the listener in a manner which allows them to be easily assimilated. They also have to be conveyed in a way which is appropriate to the 'type' of listeners the station is trying to attract, in the same way that a newspaper article will be presented to the readers to suit its readership.

One of the common complaints about broadcast sports journalists is that they deliver their lines in a condescending, childish fashion. If you get the chance to have a go at radio broadcasting, try to remember that with sport it is usually an adult audience that you are presenting to, so don't talk down to listeners or you will alienate them.

The words should be delivered as if they have just come into your head – giving the impression that you are talking accurately and knowledgeably off the cuff, but your thorough knowledge of the subject should shine through. It's comparable, in many ways, to performance sports. In gymnastics, the competitors train twice a day for years and years to build up to one big competition. They have worked incredibly hard on all the moves and have the routine carefully choreographed by specialists, but on the day of competition they make the routines look easy and natural, belying the hard work.

As a presenter, you are giving a performance in your own right and you need to sell your words to the listener by making them vibrant and lively while retaining credibility and resisting the urge to talk to listeners like they're in the playground at school.

Differences between writing for radio and writing for print

What is interesting about radio sports journalism is that although you are broadcasting to millions of sports fans, in the same way that television does, there is a huge difference in the way in which people use the two communication systems.

Groups of sports fans will sit in front of a television, or families will get together to watch matches or events, but listening to the radio tends to be a much more solitary occupation. When television commentators and announcers discuss sports events – in the studio or on the touch-lines of matches – they are addressing their audience in a different style from radio presenters, who tend to talk to their listeners as individuals.

The radio presenter needs to make each individual feel part of the larger event that he is commentating on or alluding to. Without the use of pictures this can be extremely difficult, so the presenter needs to work hard to bring colour to reports. He has to describe events, the pattern of play and the characters in great detail.

When you are writing for radio, as opposed to for magazines or newspapers, you have to write in a very different style. Because we hear things in a different way from the way in which we read them, presenters must talk logically and present facts in an order which is clear and easy to understand. There is none of the joy of running things off in a complicated order to cause people to think hard about what's been said. Newspaper journalists might be able to begin their articles with tangential statements or wise-cracks, but the radio journalist has to be aware all the time of the fact that the listeners can only follow what he says as he says it, and not go back to re-read bizarre or complicated adjuncts to the story. Skilful writing for speech is very different from newspaper writing – your words need to come in short bursts, giving just one piece of useful information at a time, and not be long, involved self-gratifying explorations of the English language!

Another key difference is that print journalists can write down the sentences as they occur to them and then change them, tidy them up, and make them neater and easier to read. Broadcast journalists have to resist the urge to neaten and sharpen sentences, because emphasis, repetition and the uneven nature of sentences will give authenticity and realism to the broadcast, which is not needed in print.

Keep remembering that your radio listener cannot review sentences in the same way that readers can, so you can repeat things without worrying too much about it – in fact, the listener will probably appreciate some repetition.

The punctuation used in print also differs immensely from that applied in radio. You need worry less about the strict interpretation of the English language, and instead write in punctuation marks in a way that will make the presentation of the piece as easy as possible. You can underline things for emphasis – use dashes instead of commas to really emphasise the pause, and have lots of short sentences and small paragraphs in order to make the piece appear to race along at a lively and interesting pace (thus reflecting the event being covered).

Finally, broadcasters have to think of the length of the piece in terms of the time it takes to say, rather than the number of words on a page. The broadcasting rule is that the average length of a one-minute broadcast is between 120 and 140 words a minute. That equates to around a quarter-page of average A4 typing (it will be half a page if you use double-spacing of course; and double-spacing is important in radio writing since you can add on particular reminders for the presenter, or notes of emphasis or pronunciation difficulties).

Preparing a broadcast tape

If you are planning to put a broadcast together yourself for an interview, or as a part of an application for a course place, the first thing to do is to work out how many words you read in a minute at a comfortable reading pace. This will enable you to tailor your writing to meet the time demands of the project you are working on.

It's worth taping yourself as you do this exercise, so that you can hear how fast you are talking in order to read that many words in the given time. If you read 200 words in a minute, then start happily multiplying that number of words by the number of minutes you have available, you may discover when you eventually come to record yourself that you are talking at a phenomenal pace and that no-one can understand you! It is much better to work out initially what speed sounds right, and how many words this implies you reading out.

If you write your piece, then discover that the number of words vastly outnumbers the required word-count for the piece, you need to cut back – but how? It's not as easy as in print journalism when you can just condense several sentences into one. In this situation, remember the rule that your prose should be flowing and should sound like you had just thought of it. It should be natural and not sound as though it has been contorted into a sentence which fits a designated brief. As such, if your piece is too long, you should cut whole sentences out or miss out one key point rather than making sentences extra long in order to fit several points into one.

Obviously, it goes without saying that talking faster is not a solution to the problem – even though it may sometimes appear to be the only answer.

What does writing for radio and writing for print have in common?

One thing which writing for all areas of the media has in common is that you need to look for *vivid* and *descriptive* ways of phrasing everything you want to say.

If you are describing the demeanour of a leading Sports Council figure in *The Times*, or discussing the fantastic last-minute goal from Paul Gascoigne in the *Sun*, you need to use all your powers of observation, creativity and description to write as effectively as possible. There is no medium where this is more vital than in radio, where the audience is totally at your mercy with regard to what the event 'looks like'. You therefore need to work hard to make sure that they can visualise the event that is taking place.

The way to best ensure that a reader can picture the event is to compare it occasionally with things that they can easy visualise. So, if you are commentating on a rugby match for radio, it would be much better to say, "Jason Leonard is running like a wild-man for the line – bursting with pride", than, "... it's Jason Leonard with the ball".

In match reports or reports of any sporting events, you need to make sure that you update people constantly on where on the pitch, on the track or in the pool the athletes are. This applies particularly to longer events like marathons, matches and long-distance swimming races, because listeners may break away from the radio broadcast to do other things, or your report may be interrupted by news updates, details of programmes coming up later, or adverts. If your report is running as part of a longer sports programme, you may find your report being broken into frequently with updates of sport results from matches going on all day around the country. Radio reporters must keep repeating the score and the details of who is playing in order to compensate for this.

Commentators have the unenviable task of having to continue commentating throughout the match even when the mike moves away from them, so that the producers can come back to the event at any time they want. Many commentators are convinced that every time they deliver a great line, make an incisive comment, or are wittier and more interesting than usual, they hear later that the mike was turned off and their moment of glory never happened!

Beyond writing

You may have proven beyond a shadow of a doubt that you have the writing and sporting skills to enable you to work in broadcasting, but in radio – unlike in print journalism, where mastery of the computer is usually the most technical aspect you have to confront – you need to be able to operate equipment in order to do your job. Even as a radio writer there is an onus on you to be able to operate fairly complicated radio equipment, and to edit your work as well as do voice-overs, add sound and produce an all-round broadcast.

It used to be the case that technicians were employed to produce the pieces and slot them all together into the required length. But in radio broadcasting today there have been many so cut-backs, and the machinery is now so transportable and simple to operate, that 'writers' are expected to manage the whole project themselves.

In sport, this is particularly true. If you are in an outside broadcast car, you will be reporting live from an event and then following up the broadcast with news stories and up-dates. After the event, you will have to get player interviews which may then need to be edited and fed back to the studio to be included in a later news programme. Even for getting into sports radio journalism in the first place, it will be of enormous help to you if you can edit your own tape, at least to a reasonable standard.

This is all a big change from the old world of radio journalism, which had infinitely more in common with television. Radio crews used to turn up like television crews with a cumbersome cavalcade following every journalist around. This was changed 50 years ago when journalists began using portable tape-recorders. It meant that suddenly journalists could get out there and do the job themselves without the necessity of a big crew. The portable tape-recorders also speeded up the process of recording and multiplied the number of places in which recordings could be made. Sports journalists before the 1940s would have had a difficult time running into changing rooms to get post-match quotes, and sneaking tape-recorders into press conferences, meetings and announcements.

The process of editing has also been speeded up by the change to magnetic tape from the slow-speed discs that were used in the past.

Doing works experience at a radio station will help to teach you the language and mechanics of the profession, and give you experience of working with modern-day equipment. Courses also provide valuable insight into the industry. Just being able to understand the language they are speaking will give you an enormous head-start.

How do you get involved in writing for radio – what are the openings?

There are five main ways in which you can get involved in radio journalism.

- Go on a radio journalism course – the National Council for the Training of Journalists will be able to give you more information, or call local colleges or your local radio station for details.
- Apply for radio jobs as they come up. Many are advertised in the *Guardian* on Mondays along with all the other media jobs. But you could also try sending letters out to radio stations to ask them where they tend to advertise their jobs; in this way you can make sure you do not miss any.
- If jobs are thin on the ground and you don't want to go on a course, the way to get experience is through doing voluntary work. Why not

contact a local radio station and explain that you would like to come in a couple of evenings a week, or go along with a radio sports presenter on a Saturday to help him in any way you can?

- If you have thought through what a radio sports journalist needs, and if you think you have an idea for a script or are convinced that you could be a great broadcaster, then you need to make a move by contacting a radio station in your area. If it's a national station that you are interested in, you need to choose the most appropriate station and contact them with a script and ideas for sports features, or offer your proven services as a sports journalist.

- Many radio sports writers start out as 'stringers', phoning copy through as stories arise and feeding in live to a news bulletin or broadcast with their version of the events at a match. You can often get work as a stringer if you are already going to an event to cover it for a newspaper or magazine. Obviously, though, you need to be careful that you file different copy to the radio station.

  If the station isn't using stringers, their sports news may be written up by a news-room journalist for the presenter to read on air. Many radio journalists remain doing this for years – or even for the rest of their careers. They become established radio journalists, but their voices are never heard by the public.

Finally, talk to your local radio stations about any possibilities of you letting them have leads every now and again – they will be only too pleased. The bottom line is, if you can get the stories, they'll use them.

Contacting a radio station

If you are contacting the station by post, then you can either send a cassette or a letter.

If you send a letter, it should be accompanied by a sample script and some evidence that you have a clue what you are doing (either evidence of your sporting knowledge or your commitment to broadcasting). Alternatively, if you are supremely confident about your abilities as a broadcaster, you could tape your script and send in the finished product. For both approaches you will need to be able to display an interest in radio sports reporting. How many leading sports radio journalists can you name? Do you know their work well, and can you distinguish between them in terms of their style as well as their voices? It really is vital that you ensure you fully understand the market-place and what good radio sports journalism is all about before you start pitching for business with a radio station. What are the sports journalists on the station that you aspire to work for like? Make sure you know all about the current reporters as well as knowing about sport and the industry generally.

Obviously, by far the largest net for freelance radio sports journalists in this country is the BBC, but there is also an increasing number of independent radio stations growing up. You will probably find that the best place to start is with your local radio station, where they may well be on the look-out for new talent. They are also more likely to be searching for local stories to fill the air-waves.

Another way of finding work is to contact a radio station that is just starting up, or has recently started. It can be very difficult for a station like Radio Kent or Radio Berkshire to put itself on the air one day, and have enough items of local interest to sustain itself for the rest of time. Initially they will relish your interest, and once you have a foot in the door you should get more work when the station's up and running.

Once you have identified a radio station that you think might be interested in your work, why not write to them and ask them for details of their scheduling as well as who are the best people to contact (obviously enclose a stamped addressed envelope).

As with print journalism, you need to make sure that you target yourself effectively. Find a niche to fit your work as well as moulding your work to fit any niche that exists. The other thing to remember is that there's no point in sending off a dramatic brief for a sports feature and addressing it to the BBC generally. You need to make enough enquiries to ensure that your piece is sent to exactly the right person.

If you opt to send in a written piece rather than a cassette, then you must be aware that your first conversation with the producer will be the assessment of your voice and your use of language over the phone. Make sure that if you have an answerphone, you sound fairly clear and logical on it; and make sure that when you talk to producers you sound crisp, clear and confident.

News versus Comment

One thing that radio stations will be relying on is your ability to understand the distinction between *news* and *comment*. If a team puts in a dreadful performance and you say that they played the worst game of their lives, this is your *comment*. It is subjective (unless there is some objective proof of it, such as someone has been quoted saying it, or it is indeed the worst result the team has ever endured).

Don't imply a judgement unless you really believe it and can back it up. It's easy on the spur of the moment to get carried away with your observations. This can be dangerous on radio where you don't get the chance to sit back when you've got your piece ready, and read it one more time before sending it. Once you have said it, there's no taking it back. You also have to remember that there is no team of subs waiting to check through your work for accuracy before it goes near the reader or listener. Once you have said something over the phone and live into a sports programme, it is too late to worry about its accuracy or impact.

Commentating

This is the most up-to-the minute, ball-by-ball way of working in radio. Good professional commentators are revered the world over; they become household names and are thought to have the most exciting and challenging jobs in broadcast sport.

The associated noises of the willow on leather, racket on ball or the crowd all go to enhance further the 'live' and action-packed nature of this exciting type of journalism. The commentator's voice represents the eyes, ears and nose of the listener as well as allowing him to add his impartial and sometime biased point of view.

Great commentators agree that the secret of good commentary is immaculate preparation. Some spend literally weeks making sure they know the name of every participant, and have crib sheets filled with every fact and figure they could possibly need during the broadcast. They work hard to try and sound as 'off the cuff' , natural and humorous as possible, but their broadcasts do have some structure to them. The way the commentator usually works is first to give the main details of the event; then, as the broadcast continues, gradually to broaden the field by adding more information. This gives greater depth and colour once the listeners have digested the basic facts. He will use every opportunity – a pause in play, a moment of little action in a race, or a gap between events – to add more detailed information about the history of the event, past results or even information about the location of the event.

Like all radio journalists, the commentator should remember that he is not always being listened to in rapt attention. Listeners will tune in and out of the radio reports as they get on with their day-to-day lives, so he should make sure that he repeats the result, score or the race leader from time to time.

Some commentators become personalities in their own right. Most of them just become expert and professional at portraying what they see on the pitch as accurately and interestingly as possible to the listeners.

Fees and copyright

Copyright

When you send off a fantastic idea to a radio station, how do you ensure that they don't just pinch it and use it themselves without paying you a penny? How indeed do you ever prove that you sent through your synopsis, idea, cassette or script? What happens if you hear your rejected script being played out later on national radio?

Luckily, radio broadcasters are protected by *copyright* once their ideas are written down in the form of a programme or script. If you merely discuss your ideas with someone, you have no legal protection if they go ahead and use them. You have only a moral code which exists between journalists to rely on. If, however, you mould these ideas into a programme, and you submit this to a radio station, you are protected without you having to take any additional action.

In the UK, or in any country that is protected by the Berne Copyright Union, you can send off your ideas and in principle you are protected. Of course, you still have the immense difficulty of proving that your work was copied. For example, if you come up with a cracking idea for a head-to-head meeting between the greatest rugby player, football player, cricketer and tennis player that ever lived; and a radio station turns you down, saying that they have already planned to do a piece like this; then you will have immense difficulty in proving they 'ripped you off'. They will simply say that they already had it in the pipe-line. In fact, since most sports feature ideas are topical – based on events happening at the moment – there is a very real chance that someone else *has* sent in exactly the same idea as you. It's a very difficult area.

So, if you have a cracking idea but you are concerned that you might be ripped off, the only way to really protect yourself is to put a sealed copy in the hands of the bank or your solicitor and obtain a dated receipt. Then, if your work is copied afterwards, you will be able to prove that you submitted it before they broadcast the feature. This will give you the first step on the road to taking action.

Whose copyright?

Even if a station buys your work you must exercise some caution over what you are selling them. When they buy your ideas or words they are buying the right to broadcast them, in the same way that a newspaper buys the right to publish. Unless you sign an 'all rights' agreement with the station, the copyright of it remains with you. You can therefore follow up the radio broadcast by extending it into a book, magazine feature or series, or by re-working it for television.

Re-working copy can be a valuable source of income, especially since once it has been accepted for broadcast, it has been given an official seal of approval by a professional – and another publication or station may therefore be keen to take it on. For this reason, be careful about signing all rights away unless it really is a one-off piece, or you think they will demand your signature before using your work.

Fees

When you first start working in broadcasting, it may seem odd that everyone seems very unwilling to discuss fees with you. Even if you ask outright, you will often be told that someone will get back to you with all the details. So until you are very well established, you may find yourself taking on a whole load of commissions without having a clue how much you will be paid for them.

This occurs for a number of reasons, but one of the primary ones is that there is still a feeling which permeates the media that working in broadcasting is a 'real treat', and that the money is secondary to the honour and prestige associated with the task. Anyone seen to be asking complicated questions about financial remuneration too early on in the negotiations will be thought to be a bit questionable, and probably not quite professional enough for the task! Obviously this varies, but many people who have started out in radio will confirm that there is still an air of this surrounding all financial negotiations.

The other problem is that the producer you talk to on a day-to-day basis about the work you're doing will not always be the right person with whom to negotiate the finer points of your contract. He will be inclined to leave all negotiations to the administration staff, who will issue you with your contract at the same time as explaining your rights and their expectations of you.

It is in your interest to get your contract *before* you start working. In this way, you are aware of the demands upon you, and of what remuneration you will receive in return. Your fee will be based on the scale of payments that they are operating, but it is unlikely that they will explain the process by which they arrived at your figure. A very rough guide to payments for sports features on national radio is £25 per minute, which means that for an average-length broadcast of four to five minutes, you will receive about £100. This might be four one-minute slots at regular intervals through a match or athletics meeting, or perhaps a continuous feature about drugs in football or violence in American football.

Obviously, you will record a lot more than four minutes' worth of material for the broadcast! In fact, if you compare the work involved with the work you would do for a match report or interview, they're fairly comparable. So you will see that unless you are a big name or being given a lot of air-time, there is not a fortune to be made in radio. The picture is much worse in local radio, where you will be extremely lucky to get any payment at all. The station is more likely to regard your contribution as work experience, and offer you a free T-shirt or station mug!

On hospital radio or voluntary sector broadcasting you would obviously not expect to be paid, and will be doing work for the experience and for something tangible to add to your CV.

Key addresses:

BBC Radio
Broadcasting House
London
W1A 1AA

BBC World Service
PO BOX 76
Bush House
Strand
London
WC2B 4PH

BBC Radio Scotland
Broadcasting House
5 Queen Street
Edinburgh
EH2 1JF

BBC Radio Wales
Broadcasting House
Llantrisant Road
Llandaff
Cardiff
CF5 2YQ

BBC Radio Ulster
Broadcasting House
Ormeau Avenue
Belfast
BT2 8HQ

BBC Radio North
New Broadcasting House
Oxford Road
Manchester
M60 1SJ

BBC Radio Midlands
Broadcasting Centre
Pebble Mill
Birmingham
B5 7QQ

BBC Radio Bristol & West
Broadcasting House
Whiteladies Road
Bristol
BS8 2LR

BBC Radio South
South Western House
Canute Road
Southampton
SO9 1PF

BBC Radio South West
Broadcasting House
Seymour Road
Mannamead
Plymouth
PL3 5BD

BBC Radio South & East
Elstree Centre
Clarendon Road
Borehamwood
Hertfordshire
WD6 1JF

BBC Radio East
St Catherine's Close
All Saints Green
Norwich
NR1 3ND

The Radio Authority
Holbrook House
14 Great Queen Street
London
WC2B 5DG

Association of Independent Radio Contractors
Radio House
46 Westbourne Grove
London
W2 5SH

Independent Radio News
200 Gray's Inn Road
London
WC1X 8YZ

11 • OTHER PUBLISHING OPPORTUNITIES

If you have tried approaching newspapers and magazines in the conventional way and keep coming up against barriers, you might think about trying some other avenue in order to get your work published.

Nine times out of ten a local newspaper, radio station or TV station will refuse to take a chance with you unless you have experience. Of course, getting experience depends on them giving you a chance – so you are immediately caught up in a 'Catch 22' situation. If you find yourself trapped in a corner like this, you might have to look at a couple of alternative ways of getting published in order to break the cycle. Even if your ultimate aim is to write for a mainstream newspaper or magazine, starting by working for a smaller publication may help you get the experience and cuttings you require to move on. Don't turn down any publishing opportunities in the early days – the more experience you've got, the better. In looking at alternative publishing opportunities, this chapter also takes a look at sports books, and at how you go about approaching a publisher with an idea for one.

In-house publications

If your company, school or college has its own newspaper or magazine, why not write for it? Most of them are desperate for contributions, and they will give you the flexibility to write whatever you want about corporate life.

The best way forward would be to contact the editor of the publication and suggest to him that you would be willing to act as sports editor. By gathering information about up-and-coming sports events, interviewing people in the company who are in the sports news, and reviewing games and sports events that have happened in your industry, you will be supplying a very real service to employees. At the same time, you are getting good cuttings and a good name for yourself, and helping the editor to fill the pages every month.

If there are no sports events going on at the company, you will have to work extra hard to think of angles (for example, if you work in insurance you might do profiles of famous sports people who have worked in insurance). You could go through up-and-coming national sports events that employees might consider watching on television or going along to. Anything, just to get a sports section up and going. Get yourself a by-line as the sports editor and do the best you can to fill the pages you are allotted with interesting articles every month.

Programmes

This is another area in which you could get publishing experience which will stand you in good stead. Local newspaper journalists will become familiar with your work if you can get a small piece in every match-day programme, and it gives you the beginnings of a cuttings file. It will also give you good contacts in the club, and the chance to test yourself editorially.

Your first step will be to approach the programme editor and offer your services for nothing. Think of new and interesting angles, and try to imagine what the average supporter really wants in his programme on match days.

If you can get yourself regular work – interviewing players for the programme, or analysing games with the coach – you will have every chance of getting a break on a local paper because your name will be familiar and your cuttings file will look good.

One-offs

Before every major sporting event, publishers put out magazines giving information on that event. These magazines are one-off titles produced just to 'soak up' the additional readers who will want to purchase a sports-specific title while an event is on.

Such publications tend to infuriate regular editors who produce magazines month-in, month-out. But the good thing about them from a freelancer's point of view is that they are often conceived quite quickly and put together by a team of people who might not know much about the specific sport. The people in the office will be working on golf one month and swimming the next, so they are to some extent in need of experts like you.

The trouble with one-offs is that it's hard to identify when they are going to come up, and who the publishers are likely to be.

The best way to proceed is to look along the book shelves and make a note of all the publishers of one-off titles. Then approach them, explaining your expertise, enclosing a CV and any other details, and asking them to contact you if they think they will need any journalists in the future.

It may prove to be fruitless, but for the effort of sending off a letter and CV you might just get lucky.

Books

Sports books used to be either biographies or coaching books. They were not well promoted, they were rarely purchased, and they lacked vision and creativity. How things have changed!

Sport is the fifth biggest industry in this country now, and publishers are producing some fiction (Nick Hornby's *Fever Pitch* is the obvious example) and plenty of non-fiction to meet the demands of this growing readership.

Around 70,000 new books are published every year, and most of these are non-fiction (a ratio of five or six to one). Today, there is considerable credibility attached to non-fiction books – it is easier to break into the market than it is to write fiction books, and there are millions of different angles that you can take in sport to provide a new and interesting read for sports fans. Sport has thousands of colourful characters, interesting stories and lively events which can form the basis for a book.

Types of non-fiction books
Biographies or Autobiographies
If you have been involved in ghosting a sportsman's column or diary in a newspaper or magazine, or if you have got to know a sportsman well and you think he's got a good story to tell, you may consider approaching publishers to find out whether they are interested in publishing it.

Paradoxically, most autobiographies are actually written by journalists – very few are written by the sports personalities themselves. The main difference between biographies and autobiographies is that the latter are written in the first person. There is always a great deal of interest in the life stories of leading sports personalities; biographies can be interesting because they are not written in the first person, so they allow the author to 'write around' the subject a little and include information from other sources to give the piece colour and life. By talking to the player's first ever coach, rivals and training partners, the writer can make the character seem alive and much fuller than by just recounting facts about the past.

Autobiographies are also very popular for different reasons. They have a genuine quality, precisely *because* they are written in the first person and so appear to be stories that are told straight from the heart. Most writers agree that first-person stories are much harder to tell, but most publishers prefer them. If you have found a likely subject and think there is a good story to tell, it would be worth giving potential publishers both options.

The main problem with writing life-story books is that in order for them to be big sellers – or indeed, even reasonably big sellers – they have to about very well-known characters. To stop them being boring, they also need to have a real 'hook' that has not really been exposed to the public until now. Unless you're a very well established journalist, or have great contacts with internationals, it can be hard to get an opportunity to write a big-name book of this nature. Further, with the increasing interest of newspapers in players' private lives, it is difficult to find a unique or revealing story that will be told through the book.

If a player will speak out for them first time about the effect the death of his baby had on his life, the terror he felt at being stalked, or his sad childhood – then you have a much more interesting story to sell to a publisher because there will be a much wider appeal than just relaying all the facts about a footballer's on-the-field action.

The other thing you have to remember when you consider writing a biography is the *timing*. There's no point in writing one if the player has been retired for a long time (unless it really is a cracking story). Remember the lead times that you're working to. By the time the book comes out, your subject may have been out of the limelight for many years.

Most biographies appear in the last year or so of a player's career, preferably pinned on to a major event that will attract publicity. For example, a particular footballer's biography might appear in World Cup year. Timing it like this gives you the opportunity to bring out a paperback version of the book, with an additional chapter up-dating readers on the tournament that has just passed. It may even give you the chance to do an autobiography a year later when the player announces his retirement.

Agents are very often used to negotiate the best deals, so you may like to try and track one down if you think it's necessary. For help with this, refer to the *Writers' & Artists' Yearbook*, published by A&C Black.

Historical books

Every major sports event is marked by dozens of magazine articles, books and 'one-off' publications which spring up to record it. These can range from picture-led, glossy coffee-table books outlining the best moments of the Olympics, to detailed statistics from the badminton World Championships; from *100 Years of Football* to a history of women's sport or sport in schools. There might even be a local club that is celebrating an anniversary, so that you consider there might be some local interest in a book about the club.

Comment books

Sport provokes strong reactions in people, and many leading journalists feel motivated to write books such as those which analyse 'the 40 days that changed the fabric of the sport' or look at the sociological issues in a sport (drugs, or football hooliganism).

Guide books

These might focus on an event (a guide to the Olympics, for example, featuring details of the sportsmen to look out for and a full guide to the TV coverage), or on a tournament or club. They could offer a guide to the Five Nations Rugby Championships, to sport in the north-east, or to the gymnastics clubs in England and Wales.

Guide books differ from historical books in that they are written before the event. The important thing to remember is that in order to be on the shelves a couple of months before the event, they are written a year or so before and commissioned much earlier than that. Don't wait until an event is on your doorstep before contacting a publisher, because they will either already have the publication already commissioned, or it will be far too late to do anything about it.

Coaching or playing manuals

Sport enthusiasts have cupboards full of books such as *Improve Your Golf Swing* or *Change Your Running Style in 30 Easy Steps*. If you know a great deal about the practical side of sport, and can back this up with either an authoritative qualification or experience, then you might fancy having a go. The difficulty is in finding an area to write about that is not too narrow (i.e., that is of interest to so few people that it's not worth doing). The more you broaden your initial idea to make it more marketable, the more chance there is that a book of the same nature is already sitting on the shelves somewhere.

If you intend to write a coaching book, bear one thing in mind: for it to be successful, it has to be new or better than everything else on the market.

Many coaching books these days – particularly those directed at children – are written in conjunction with a celebrity. A good example is Gary Lineker's *Soccer Skills* book.

Light-hearted sports books

These might be compilations of embarrassing or silly moments in sport – players' stories about the daft things they've done on tour, on the pitch or in the bar. The trouble with such books is that stories that were very funny at the time can translate badly on to paper and do not read as if the stories were very funny at all. They work best if you can get a celebrity to put his name to the book: for example, John MacEnroe's *Tennis Howlers*.

It may also take a disproportionate amount of work to get hold of interesting stories to include. Always start your research before committing to a publisher for a book of this nature.

Coming up with an idea

There is no point in just having some sort of abstract desire to write a book. Most people, if you asked them, would express a similar interest. But to be able to sit down and write between 70,000 and 80,000 words about a subject demands a thorough knowledge and passion in that subject area.

Is there something in which you have an over-riding interest? If so, is it a marketable subject area? Are other people likely to be interested in it?

Take the subject you are interested in and break it down into sub-topics. These can be periods in a sportsman's life, different games to feature in a 'Greatest Games' book, or stages in an event or sport if you are doing an historical book. At this stage it will become apparent whether you really have enough knowledge or material to write extensively on each of these areas. You will obviously find that you know much more about one area than another, but do you have enough knowledge about all the separate components to put the book together well? Even if you can satisfy yourself that you could write this book well, will people want to read it? You need to be clear about *why* you are writing the book, and about who you think will buy it before you approach a publisher with an idea.

You also need to think about *how many* people are likely to buy the book. You have to ensure that, however specialist the book is, you will still get a good few thousand people wanting to buy it. If you think that your idea is perhaps a little too narrow for genuine mainstream interest, then you could work with another writer who has a specialism of his own. Together, you may be able to produce something with more commercial appeal. For example, if you are a baseball coach with enormous knowledge about hitting the ball, and you want to write a book about the 'hit' in baseball – including all the attendant information about the bio-mechanics of the moment of contact, the swing and the stance – you may find that this book on its own is not really likely to succeed because of the narrowness of its appeal. However, there may be a chance of getting a book about 'the hit' generally published, so you may consider getting together with a cricket and rounders expert to produce a joint venture.

Putting a sales package together

Once you have thought through your original germ of an idea, and are convinced that you have a marketable book on your hands, it is time to go about selling the idea to a publisher.

To sell to a publisher you need to produce a basic synopsis of the areas you think the book will address. Whilst you need to be as professional as possible from the beginning, don't worry too much about the exact content of the synopsis since it will change several times before you eventually make it into print. The aim of your initial synopsis is to sell the idea to a publisher in the first place.

In addition to enclosing a synopsis of the book, you need to answer several key questions for the publisher. These questions are best summed up by the old adage: who, why, what, where and when.

- *Who* is the book aimed at? Who will go out and buy the book? You need to have a clear idea of the sort of people who will want it.
- *Why* are you writing it? Is there a gap in the market? Is there a much better way in which you can envisage writing the book?
- *What* will the book include? Most of this will be covered by the synopsis, but its worth summing it up in a couple of paragraphs for the publisher to glance at.
- *Where* will you do your research, get all your information? Where will the facts and figures come from?
- *When* will you get the book finished by? Try to be as accurate as possible. Think clearly about your own work commitments as well as when would be the best time to put a book like the one you are proposing out into the market-place.

The other thing that a publisher will be interested to know about is you. *Why* should *they* commission *you* to write the book? You need to show that you have the necessary writing skills, experience and knowledge to make a good job of it. To do this, you might consider enclosing a CV, cuttings and a covering letter outlining the project you are proposing, explaining what your qualities and experiences are and why you are the right person for the job.

Finding a publisher

Once you have your package together – breaking down your book idea (the synopsis), including a letter which explains your personal qualities and the broad aims of the book, and enclosing some cuttings or a CV (if relevant) and a page breakdown of the marketing of the book (who is it aimed at, etc.) – then you need to send the whole package off to a publisher.

At this stage, many people will send the package off to dozens of publishers at one time. There is nothing particularly wrong with this approach, and it will certainly save you months of sitting around and waiting for an individual publisher to make up his mind, but it does mean extra work for you. It may also lead to some problems if more than one publishing house expresses an interest at the same time.

A better way to proceed is to identify the 'right publisher' at the beginning, so you can send it to just one at a time. One way to find the right publisher is to look at the books on your own shelf, or visit a library and assess which publishers publish which books. Is there is a publisher who seems to be publishing books like the one you propose writing? If so, send it off to them, and say why you have approached them in the covering letter. For example:

> "I thought you may be interested in the enclosed proposal for *Learning to Bat*, because it would appear to sit neatly into your current portfolio which includes *Learning to Swim*, and *Learning to Ski*."

Coping with rejection

Remember that publishers get dozens of book ideas sent into them every day, and you may have been turned down for a simple reason: it's not the right book for them; the timing is bad; they have just committed all their finances for the year; or you have sent it to the wrong person in the company.

Most publishers are good at giving you at least an inkling of why they have turned you down – especially if they see how much effort you have gone to with the proposal. However, if you just get a standard letter back from the publishers rejecting your synopsis, it would be worth sending a letter and stamped addressed envelope back to ask them why you were rejected. It is important not to take rejection too seriously – use the criticism you get to adapt your proposal and send it somewhere else.

12 • THE FREELANCE BUSINESS

Introduction

It seems terribly laborious to think about fax machines and floppy disks when all you really want to do is envisage yourself as sport's modern-day answer to Oscar Wilde – strutting around dispensing shrewd and witty observations on the world of sport. But the fact is that if you want to work as a full-time freelance journalist, then you are effectively running a business – the business of providing the right words in the right quantity to the right place by the right time.

As such, there are certain business skills that you can effectively employ to ensure that everything runs smoothly. Even if you are just doing a bit of freelancing at the weekend and you think of it as being little more than a hobby while you continue to run a full-time job during the week, you will find that combining the two becomes much less hassle if you take the same business approach to the latter as you do to the former.

Correspondence

Be as professional as you can in all your correspondence. You may decide that this means you have to purchase expensive office equipment and it may mean nothing more than buying some new envelopes.

Indeed, when you're first starting out it would be unwise to make a massive initial investment in equipment. As long as you have a telephone, answering-machine and somewhere that you can write legible letters and the articles you are commissioned to produce, you have all the tools you need to become a writer. You can come over as being professional and competent without a plethora of impressive office facilities. It's only later on, when you're starting to think about writing books and longer pieces regularly, that you may think seriously about investing some of your income in business equipment. It's important to remember when you do purchase this equipment that if it is for work purposes, you can claim the price of it back against the tax you have to pay.

The professional attitude you display in your letters and your articles should be extended to all areas of the freelance business, from sending in invoices to managing your accounts for tax purposes. If you make sure that the correct invoices are going in to the right department with all the relevant information on them, you will have far more chance of being paid properly and on time than if you make a series of check-calls to the wrong department when you suddenly remember that you haven't been paid – three weeks later!

It's also vital that you have a rough idea of what your incomings and out-goings are so you don't get caught out by paying too much or too little tax.

This chapter will take you through the key areas to think of when you are setting up in business as a full-time freelance, or just making some extra money on the side by covering the occasional sports event. It is by no means an exhaustive guide, but there are plenty of good publications on the market which deal specifically with this area, so if you are thinking of pursuing a career as a freelancer, it would be well worth visiting the local library to browse through some of them. If you need specific advice on tax issues, try contacting your local tax office direct. They do a series of leaflets and book-lets which should be of more specific use to you than a generic book.

The 'pros and cons' of working as a full-time freelancer

Trend analysers are adamant that the way forward for the work-force is into a freelance lifestyle. Terminology like 'down-shifting' is used to explain the movement of people out of London and into the country where they can work in the comfort of their own homes.

However, when it comes to writing it can be very difficult to make enough money working as a full-time freelancer, so many people keep on other jobs – on local papers, in libraries, colleges or as teachers – while they pursue their interest as a writer.

If you have put together a business plan, if you know exactly what you need to achieve to meet all your financial targets, and if you are convinced that you can meet them, it still does not mean that a freelance lifestyle will be the right thing for you. Though you may be fed up with playing corporate politics and long for a freer lifestyle, going freelance is a huge change – and one that can leave you feeling unmotivated and lonely.

Motivation

You have to be extremely self-motivated to sit in your house with a million things to do all around you, and ignore them all to write your book or article. Since you're not in a work environment, it's easy to wander around the house and start watching television, getting yourself something to eat or doing housework.

If you can have a separate room which acts as your office, this will help immensely. It will enable you to associate one area of your house with your writing, so that when you want a break you can leave the room, and when you are ready to continue you can go back into it. That way you will have one area of your house that feels like an office, and you may be able to convince yourself to treat it like one.

Flexibility

It is important to remember that although you may feel as if you're escap-ing from the rigidity and inflexibility of a 9–5 work schedule when you go freelance, you are in fact still answerable to those people you are writing for. They are on the end of the telephone, and just as likely to be fussy and set unreasonable deadlines as someone you used to work for in the office.

The other thing that can be difficult when you go freelance is that your day-to-day interaction with other people – all the conversations and discussions you used to have, many of which sparked off ideas for features – will dry up. The result of this is that thinking of ideas for features, and having your finger on the pulse of what people out there really feel, can be much more difficult.

On the plus side, being freelance means that you can do work that generates more work. For example, you can easily get to cover sporting events. If you used to work from 9.00 a.m. until 5.00 p.m. for an employer, and then freelance at the weekends, it was probably very difficult to get to mid-week sporting events on the other side of the country. It might have involved taking half the day off work. As a freelancer, you suddenly have the freedom and flexibility to attend matches, competitions and tournaments as they arise.

Managing your business

Once you have set yourself up as a writer – whether doing part-time freelance projects or full-time sports writing – there will be a million and one things that you can buy to make running the business much easier. Only you can decide whether you really need them, or whether they're a luxury that you can realistically do without. One thing you do need to consider is: where are you going to write? It's ideal to have an office, or at least a desk at home that you can work from; but if you don't have this luxury, make sure you identify your own space where you can work and leave your things lying around when you need to, without fear of them being moved around by someone.

Office stationery

Obviously, as a writer you will need an ample supply of paper, notebooks, pencils and pens. Whether you decide to invest in personal stationery depends on whether you think having the stationery will give you a more business-like look which will affect your ability to pull in big commissions. The answer, nine times out of ten, is that it won't. One nice thing about being a writer is that people can see instantly whether you can do the job. There's something tangible that prospective employers can look at to see whether you have the ability – your portfolio.

However, many of your sports contacts will be made in bars, social clubs and sporting clubs, and you may feel that having a set of business cards to dish out whenever you meet contacts will enhance your chances of getting a call from people afterwards. You can get cards made up fairly cheaply with your name, address and telephone number on, then you can attach them when you are sending off cuttings, CVs, letters and articles, as well as having them to hand out to contacts.

If you are keen to invest in some office stationery, cards may be of more general use to you initially than letter-headed paper.

Cuttings

You need to make sure that you keep up-to-date with everything that is going on in your sport. One great way to do this is to keep newspaper cuttings of everything you see, and invest some of your work-time into keeping this cuttings file up-to-date and filed in alphabetical or chronological order so that you can easily find clips when you want them.

For example, if you are an athletics correspondent for a couple of local papers, it would be worth tearing out and keeping any features on athletics that you see, and filing them in an expanding file. Have a separate envelope for each leading athlete, or for each issue or club in the sport; then when you find a cutting on that subject, just slot it into the appropriate envelope. This is then filed back in the expanding file under the appropriate letter.

A filing system like this is useful in many respects. First, it gives you a catalogue of information about everything that's been going on in your sport, so that if a major national issue suddenly has a bearing on a local sports club you will be able to look back at the wider national picture for reference. Then, if a top athlete like Roger Black is coming to run a session at a local club and you want to do an interview with him, you will have a ready-made file of information from which to research the interview. The final reason for keeping a file like this is that you can keep copies of work by all the top journalists. You can look through these and learn about different journalism styles and approaches; this will be extremely useful to you if you have aspirations to write for a national paper. By studying the writers who have the jobs you want, and by looking at the way in which they structure their report and features, you will learn how different they all are. You will also see how they have clear individual styles that set them apart from the thousands of other writers who are keen to work at the highest levels.

The other cuttings file that you will need is the one which contains all your own work. However far advanced you are in your career, having a record of the work you've done to date will be invaluable in proving to new publications that you have the experience and ability to do a good job for them.

Most good stationers will sell proper portfolios (often called *display books*). Alternatively, just stick your cuttings into a scrap-book. Remember, though, that if all your articles are stuck in a pile of scrap-books you may want to collect the ones that you are particularly proud of and keep them separately in a display book – in case you need to show them to anyone.

Generating work

This is where many freelance journalists come unstuck! When you first start as a full-time freelancer, money will be coming in erratically – but you need regular access to it. Work may rush in suddenly so that you find yourself inundated with jobs, but if you are going to succeed you still need to find time to generate more work for the next month, and make long-term plans for work in the months ahead. If you just sit back and cover the work that comes in without spending some time thinking of articles that you can write next month, you will soon find yourself in dire straits the next month when there is no work around.

Payment

So, you've come up with a great idea. It's been accepted by an editor, you have been commissioned to write the piece, and everything's done. How do you bring up the difficult subject of payment? And how do you manage your business so that you can keep track of future commissions, keep coming up with ideas and make sure payments come in on time? The answer is to commit some time to managing your books and making sure you think of it as an important area of your business life.

Payment arrangements vary as much from publication to publication as the stories you write for them. On many papers and magazines there is a set fee and there is no chance at all of you being able to negotiate a different arrangement. If you are determined to set a figure yourself for the work you do, you may be in for a disappointing time – such papers or magazines may choose to use someone else instead of you.

On local papers in particular you may find yourself working for nothing, or perhaps just for expenses, in order to get your foot on to the ladder. Once you have found a niche for yourself on the paper, then you might be in a position to talk to the sports editor about some remuneration and perhaps even the chance to get more involved in the publication in terms of ident-ifying key stories that are coming up, discussing feature ideas and developing the section you are working on. If you can build up your profile you'll give yourself more ammunition for your portfolio, particu-larly if you can get yourself a title – perhaps athletics correspondent or staff rugby writer. Then, the next time you are searching out work it just may fall to your advantage. Editors are very busy people, and they get dozens of portfolios and letters in every week. If your letter and CV announce that you have already risen to the dizzy heights of athletics correspondent, it just may tip the balance between whether an editor pushes your letter automatically to one side or whether he reads on a little further and perhaps offers you the chance to do some work for the magazine or paper.

The best way to proceed is to ask up front what you are likely to be paid. However, be cautious about appearing too determined to make as much money as possible. Remember that editors are inundated with people writing and phoning with ideas every week, and most of them are happy to work for nothing. It's the curse of being a writer that the profession is so popular. Writers willing to work for nothing lower the rates that editors are willing to pay, so that the industry as a whole has become devalued.

A general rule is to be prepared to work for nothing more than expenses to start with, if you think it's the best way of getting a portfolio together. Once you have ascertained that you can do a good job, and are worth taking seriously, talk to the sports editor about finances before you are taken for granted. On specialist magazines and local newspapers the fees you can expect will be extremely small compared to those paid by consumer magazines and big selling tabloid newspapers. If you want to get a rough idea of the range of freelance rates, the NUJ will supply a list of them – but at the end of the day, the publication will pay you what they have decided their rates are, and if you don't want to work under their conditions they'll find plenty of people who will. Editorial work is badly paid on the whole, precisely because there are so many people eager to work. If you become a 'name' and are sought after by newspapers and magazines, then clearly you have more bargaining power than if you are starting out and are desperate to get a by-line.

The key to making money from freelancing is often to take the small regular commissions, so that you know you have a regular amount coming in each month. Then start looking for bigger commissions, but *never* let down your regular contacts because they don't pay as much. At the end of the day, the regular, solid work is vital and acts as a comfort zone from which you can seek out additional work. In fact, it can take so long to send ideas back and forth to a glossy magazine, and then send your cuttings off and go in to see the editor, that building up a small network of local newspaper contacts can mean that for the amount of time you spend on it, local newspaper work can be more rewarding financially.

Payment and Overheads

When you are working freelance, you have to consider the cost of putting an article together as well as the income you will receive. These are not direct costs like travel which should be reimbursed in expenses, but costs like heating, lighting and equipment. If you consider that your overheads amount to a cost of £1 per hour, a chargeable rate for a job might be £10 per hour (comprising the £1 overhead payment, £7 salary and £2 profit). Obviously, when you are working for a newspaper or magazine you will be paid a set fee for the job; but it may be worth keeping in the back of your mind what your hourly rate of achievement should be to meet the needs of your business.

It also may help you to be more discerning when you are in a position to choose what work you do. Work which seems instantly more profitable may actually turn out to be infinitely less profitable when you calculate the hours involved, particularly if it involves a great deal of travelling.

Of course, you have to weigh up the value of doing each job in terms of the contacts it produces and the prestige within the industry which it creates; but you do also have to look at the commercial implications if you are ever going to make the business side of writing a success.

When will you be paid, and what if payments don't come through?

Journalists' payments are usually made once the edition in which the work appears is out. Magazines – and in particular monthlies – work a long way ahead, so that if you are commissioned in August to write a piece for the December or January issue, you may not actually receive payment until some time in February – six months after you sent the story in. Obviously, if you have a number of projects on the go at any one time the money will be coming in regularly; but if you are just starting out, be prepared to have to wait for payment.

Expenses

Whilst writing is a relatively low-cost business, you still need to record your costs carefully since several of them may be claimable from the publication you write for. If your work for them involves a long trip or having lunch with someone, you may be able to send in expenses with your invoice – check this with them beforehand. Alternatively, if you can't claim the money from your employer, you may well be able to claim against income tax.

Your expenses will be divided into two broad areas: *overheads* and *direct costs*. Overheads are costs that you incur continuously – the costs of running the business. They might include rent or mortgage, rates, telephone, stationery, secretarial assistance, business equipment and car running costs. Direct costs are only incurred on a specific job, and might include photographer's fees, research documents, special travelling or any other materials relating to the job.

Both overheads and direct costs need to be taken into account when you assess your profitability,

Tax

Remember that the money you receive will not be taxed, and that you will have to declare the tax on any income, so you need to sort out paying tax separately. You should also keep a note of expenses that you incur in the writing of articles because these can be claimed back against your tax bill.

If you start to earn a considerable amount of money through writing, you may want to employ an accountant who will look after your books for you. The fee that you pay an accountant can also be claimed back against tax, so this may be worth considering. You need to weigh up how much money you will save by using an accountant compared to how much an accountant will cost you. Fees vary enormously between accountants, so it is advisable to shop around or ask fellow journalists to recommend someone.

The amount of income tax you pay is based on your profits – on the difference between the income you accrue through writing and your allowable business expenses.

If you work from home, you can claim part of your domestic running expenses – around 25%. You should include gas and electricity bills, together with a proportion of the telephone rental charge (individual calls would be a direct cost). You can also claim all the costs of running the business, such as stationery, computer disks, postage, and subscriptions to professional bodies. Travelling costs can only be claimed if they are exclusively for business. If you use a car for business you need to record your total mileage and your genuine business mileage. What you can then claim is a percentage of all the car running costs, including petrol, road tax, insurance and maintenance.

Office Equipment

It is becoming increasingly difficult for journalists and authors to work without computers. At most matches and sports events, journalists will need to start recording the day's events before the end of the meeting, and bashing away at a portable computer is the easiest and most time-efficient way of doing it.

Book publishers and magazines will often ask for copy on disk; and in the case of daily newspapers, they may well change the word-count they require from you at some stage during the day if a major sports story breaks requiring more room on the page. In such a situation, you need to be able to amend your story quickly. If it's in your note-book or has been bashed out on a typewriter, then it will be much more difficult to adapt than if it is stored on a computer disk.

If you can afford a computer – and remember that business expenses can be set against tax – think carefully about which package to buy. Talk to your key publications about which systems they use, so you can make sure you are compatible with as many as possible.

Once you have a computer it's much easier to keep everything in order. You can have a separate disk for each publication that you work for, and even invest in an accounts package or management package at some stage if you feel the need to organise yourself more effectively.

Whilst most writers like to think of themselves as being immersed in a very creative and elusive art, the scientific and mechanical back-up that is now available from computers can be vital to producing the required word-length to the required specification by the required date. Even authors who like to write while tucked away in a tree-covered hide-away need, ultimately, to be practical about getting their words from their head on to the page in the easiest way possible. This is invariably through a word processor. There are hundreds of them on show in shops. But before you can start to work out which word processor will best suit your requirements, and what specific functions you need on the computer, you need to talk to the publications that you most regularly file copy for. If they work on Apple Macintosh computers, and you want to be able to send through words via a modem system, then there really is no point in buying a totally incompatible system.

Many publications will ask for anything other than short news items to be on disk, so check that you will be able to provide disks that they can read on their computers – or the very reason for which you bought your computer in the first place may turn out to be inherently flawed.

Computer functions

There are certain functions that a computer performs which are particularly useful to a journalist. The spell-check is the most obvious, and it really is useful if you're bashing away on the computer in a hurry and want to check how many 'S's are in a word without digging out your dictionary.

The thesaurus is another useful tool. If you read through your copy and find that you have used the same word twice, and if you cannot think of an alternative, then the thesaurus may be able to help you out.

The spell-check and thesaurus now appear in most computer packages, but it is worth checking first, because you will add extra costs on if you have to buy additional software later.

Telephones, faxes and modems

It is vital that you are easily contactable if you are a freelancer. Obviously a phone at home, or in your place of work, is an essential item; but you may also wish to consider investing in mobile phones, bleepers, pagers or any other example of the multitude of communication gadgets around.

If you are covering sports events for a newspaper, you may need to phone through results and copy throughout the game. In this case you will find a mobile phone useful, especially if you tend to go to sporting grounds where access to telephones is difficult to come by.

A fax machine is another piece of equipment which is extremely useful, especially if you have quite lengthy magazine articles to deliver. Many magazine offices have a small staff and would be reluctant to tie up one of the members of staff in taking copy over the phone from you.

If you are covering events abroad, or are sending in a great deal of copy on a regular basis, then a modem might be an alternative. With a modem, your copy is transmitted directly on the computer screen without it having to be keyed in the other end, so it is a great time saver. It also means that few typographical errors are committed in the process of relaying the information. Obviously, the downside of such technology is that it requires investment up front, which can be difficult.

Sporting Equipment

When you go to sporting events there is some equipment that will be useful to you. Number one is the press pass, a must if you can get hold of one because it will help you gain entry to matches and events. Contact the NUJ for more information.

Basic tools

Once you arrive in the press box, you will need to make sure that you have with you a note-book and a couple of pens. If you are writing a colour piece as well as keeping a note of scorers and match statistics, it may be worth bringing a separate pad, or a separate piece of paper to record stats on while you scribble the main body text into your note-book.

Helpful additional tools

In addition to the obvious, you may also consider taking binoculars if you think you may be some way from the event. These are particularly useful if you are writing a blow-by-blow account of the action, and need to know details of exactly what was wrong with a gymnast's somersault or describe a fielder's catch in great detail.

A stop-watch can also be useful, particularly if you are reporting blow-by-blow on a match. You may need to report that in the nineteenth minute, someone scored. The only reliable way to do this is to take your own stop-watch and carefully make notes of when key goals and significant moments occur.

You may also want to take with you to the match any relevant cuttings or books for references, particularly if an unknown athlete comes through and you want to be able to include details about him in your piece.

Advanced tools

Finally, if you have one, a portable computer and a mobile phone are both useful at sports events. If you are filing teams before the events, copy at the half-way point, and then a final analysis, it can help immensely to have the information stored away in a computer. Having a mobile phone might be the only way in which you have access to a telephone, unless you have been able to book one in advance.

The Law

Libel

Libel is the trickiest aspect of the law for journalists to deal with, and sports writers are becoming increasingly entangled in the complicated legal web as sport as an industry grows.

The law of libel exists to protect the reputation of the individual from unjustified attacks. The law covers moral and professional reputation. As more and more sportsmen are becoming professionals and deriving their main source of income from their sport, so your words about a player may harm his professional reputation more than they would have 20 years ago when sport was performed much more for pleasure than as an occupation.

The fact that there are so many sports lawyers around, with firms specialising in sports law springing up everywhere, gives an indication of how important the field is now.

As sport becomes a bigger and bigger industry, there are more and more ways in which professional reputations can be damaged. If a millionaire backs a local club and there is simultaneously a great deal of ill-feeling locally because 'someone with a seedy reputation' is involved, you have to be extremely careful what you write – even if you are just reflecting local opinion.

Most publications will have an arrangement with a lawyer, or may even have in-house lawyers who will look through copy that may result in a libel claim. However, as a freelance writer you have to make sure that you have done your best to avoid producing copy that is unbalanced or unjustifiable. If you want to write something contentious and are worried about the effects that it will have, it is well worth drawing the piece to the attention of the sports editor when you submit it.

In order for someone to succeed in a libel case, he needs to be able to prove three things:

1. A defamatory statement was made about him.
2. It is reasonably understood that the statement referred to him.
3. It has been published to a third person.

A statement is said to be *defamatory* if it:

1. Exposes him to hatred, ridicule or contempt.
2. Causes him to be shunned or avoided.
3. Lowers him in the estimation of right-thinking members of society generally.
4. Disparages him in his office, profession or trade.

Even if you are quoting something that someone else has said, you could still find yourself on the receiving end of a writ. The person who said the original statement may be liable, but anyone who repeats the allegation may also be sued. Indeed, a person who has been defamed may sue the reporter, the sub-editor, the editor and the publishing company! But it's not all doom and gloom. If a manager says that one of his players is not worthy of his place, and is unfit and a bad team player, you can use the quote if you think you can defend yourself.

The law of defamation tries to strike a balance between the individual's right to have his reputation protected, and freedom of speech. If you are exposing massive corruption or drug taking at a swimming club, you are allowed to expose these wrong-doings as long as you remember what you may be forced to prove in court.

The defences you have against a libel writ are:

- *Justification* – a complete defence to a libel action. You have to prove that the words complained of are true in substance and in fact. This defence applies to facts. If the complaint is about the expression of an opinion, your defence may be:
- *Fair Comment* – is a plea that the matter complained of is fair comment made in good faith and without malice on a matter of public interest. The facts underlining the comment have to be true for this defence to work.
- *Privilege* – this covers occasions that the law has understood should be given complete freedom of speech. It is divided into *absolute privilege* and *qualified privilege*. For example, in Parliament there is absolute privilege for the members to say whatever they choose; but reports of Parliamentary debates only have qualified privilege, which means that the motive for publishing will be examined. In qualified privilege, anything can be printed as long as it is fair and accurate and written without malice.
- *Unintentional Defamation* –this is when a journalist invents a fictitious character in a story to give the piece some colour, then a real person by the same name comes forward and sues; or if the writer defames someone because he writes something which appears innocuous, but because of reasons unknown to him it is defamatory.

    For example, if a photograph came into the office of a footballer standing next to a woman, and it was captioned 'John Smith and his fiancée', there would be nothing libellous in this, However, if the player turned out to be married, his wife may sue on the grounds that her reputation had been damaged because people who knew her assumed she was living in sin.

Rights

Many magazines will ask to buy rights to your articles at the commissioning stage, and it is well worth you being aware of exactly what rights you are giving them to your intellectual property.

A magazine or newspaper may well send through a commissioning form which you are asked to send back. The form will confirm in writing what you have agreed over the phone, and it will outline how much you are being paid and when the copy is due in. The form may also state that the company is buying *All Rights, First Use* or *Qualified Rights*.

Since sport is a global concern, it is often the case that publications will want to buy all rights to your work so that they can syndicate it around the world and make money for the publication. If you give them qualified rights, it means that you will receive a percentage of any sell-ons of your story. First British usage means that the magazine is buying a one-off use of the article but that you are free to sell it on elsewhere.

There's really no point in putting 'First British Serial Rights' on the top of an article, as many new freelancers do. If they buy all rights, you are committed to handing the whole thing over to them.

Remember when granting all rights to your work that this may include the electronic media as well.

It is well worth being clear about the rights form you are signing, particularly if you have a big story. But also be aware that unless you have a real scoop on your hands, or a top celebrity interview, re-sale may not amount to a fantastic amount in any case.

APPENDIX

THE ADDRESS BOOK

The Sports Council
16 Upper Woburn Place
London
WC1H OQP

Tel: 0171-273 1500
Fax: 0171-383 5740

National Union of Journalists
Acorn House
314 Gray's Inn Road
London
WC1X 8DP

Tel: 0171-278 7916
Fax: 0171-837 8143

Association of Freelance Journalists
5 Beacon Flats
Kings Haye Road
Wellington
Telford
Shropshire
TF1 1RG

British Association of Journalists
88 Fleet Street
London
EC4Y 1PJ

Tel: 0171-353 3003
Fax: 0171-353 2310

The Sports Writers' Association
16 Upper Woburn Place
London
WC1H OQP

Tel: 0171-273 1500
Fax: 0171-383 5740

National Council for the Training of Journalists
Tel: 01279-430009

National Coaching Foundation
114 Cardigan Road
Headingly
Leeds
LS6 3BJ

Tel: 01532-744802

Sports Council Publications
PO Box 255
Wetherby
West Yorkshire
LS23 7LZ

Tel: 0990-210255
Fax: 0990-210266

Central Council for Physical Recreation
Francis House
Francis Street
LONDON
SW1P 1DE

Tel: 0171-828 3163

Hayters Sports Agency
4–5 Gough Square
London
EC4A 3DE

Tel: 0171-837 7171

Women's Sports Foundation

Tel: 0171-831 7863

SPORTS GOVERNING BODIES

Aikido

Mrs S Timms
Secretary
British Aikido Board
6 Halkingcroft
Langley
Slough
SL3 7AT

Home tel: 01753-819086

American Football

Mr D Quincey
League Commissioner
British American Football
Association
22A Market Place
Still Lane
Boston
Lincs
PE21 6EH

Tel: 01205-363 522
Fax: 01205-358 139

Angling

Mr K E Watkins
Chief Administrative Officer
National Federation of
Anglers
Halliday House
Eggington Junction
Derby
DE65 6GU

Tel: 01283-734735
Fax: 01283-734799

Mr D E Rowe
Development Officer
National Federation of Sea
Anglers
51A Queen Street
Newton Abbot
Devon TQ12 2QJ

Tel: 01626-331330
Fax: 01626-331330

Mr C Poupard
Director
Salmon and Trout
Association
Fsihmongers Hall
London Bridge
London
EC4R 9EL

Tel: 0171-283 5838
Fax: 0171-929 1389

Archery

Mr J S Middleton
Chief Executive
Grand National Archery
Society
Seventh Street
National Agricultural
Centre
Stoneleigh
Kenilworth
Warwickshire
CV8 2LG

Tel: 01203-696631
Fax: 01203-419662

Mr C Aston
National Contact
National Crossbow
Federation of Great Britain
9 Manor Street
Upper Green
Tettenhall
Wolverhampton
W Midlands
WW6 8RA

Tel: 01902-758870

Arm Wrestling

Mr D Shead
British Arm Wrestling
Federation
Unit 4 Gym
Nettlefold Place
London SE27 0JW

Tel: 0181-761 0597

Association Football

Ms H Gevons
Coordinator for Women's
Football
Football Association
9 Wyllyotts Place
Potters Bar
Herts
EN6 2JD

Tel: 01707-651840
Fax: 01707-644190

Mr G Kelly
Chief Executive
Football Association, The
16 Lancaster Gate
London
W2 3LW

Tel: 0171-262 4542
Fax: 0171-402 0486

Athletics

Mr R Mitchell
Honorary Secretary
Amateur Athletic
Association of England
225A Bristol Road
Edgbaston
Birmingham
B5 7UB

Tel: 0121-440 5000
Fax: 0121-440 0555

Professor P. Radford
Executive Chairman
British Athletic Federation
225A Bristol Road
Edgbaston
Birmingham
B5 7UB

Tel: 0121-440 5000
Fax: 0121-440 0555

Badminton

Mr G Snowdon
Chief Executive
Badminton Association of
England
National Badminton Centre
Bradwell Road
Loughton Lodge
Milton Keynes
Bucks
MK8 9LA

Tel: 01908-568822
Fax: 01908-566922

Ballooning

Mr D Belton
Secretary
British Balloon and Airship
Club
Forde Abbey Farm House
Chard
Somerset
TA20 4LP

Home Tel: 01460-220880

Baseball

Mr K Macadam
Administration Secretary
British Baseball Federation
66 Belvedere Road
Hessle
N Humberside
HU13 9JJ

Tel: 01482-643551
Fax: 01482-640224

Basketball

Mr S Catton
Chief Executive
English Basketball
Association
48 Bradford Road
Stanningley
Pudsey
W Yorkshire
LS28 6DF

Tel: 0113-236 1166
Fax: 0113-236 1022

Bicycle Polo – see Cycling

Billiards and Snooker

Mr N Oldfield
Operations Executive
World Professional Billiards
and Snooker Association
27 Oakfield Road
Clifton
Bristol
BS8 2AT

Tel: 0117-974 4491
Fax: 0117-974 4931

Bobsleigh

Ms H Alderman
Secretary
British Bobsleigh
Association
85 High Street
Codford
Warminster
Wilts
BA12 0ND

Tel: 01985-850064
Fax: 01985-850064

Boccia

Mrs M Wagstaff
Administrator
National Boccia Association
11 Churchill Park
Colwick
Nottingham
NG4 2HF

Tel: 0115-940 1202

Bowls

Mr R Holt
Secretary
British Crown Green
Bowling Association
14 Leighton Avenue
Maghull
Liverpool
L31 0AH

Tel: 0151-526 8367

Mr D W Johnson
Secretary
English Bowling Association
Lyndhurst Road
Worthing
W Sussex
BN11 2AZ

Tel: 01903-820222
Fax: 01903-820444

Mr J Heppel
Secretary
English Bowling Federation
62 Frampton Place
Boston
Lincs
PE21 8EL

Tel: 01205-366201

Mr D Brown
Secretary
English Indoor Bowling
Association
David Cornwell House
Bowling Green
Leicester Road
Melton Mowbray
Leics
LE13 0DB

Tel: 01664-481900

Mr N Dickenson
Secretary
English Short Mat Bowling
Association
10 Bradley Close
Middlewich
Cheshire
CW10 0PF

Mrs M Ruff
Secretary
English Women's Indoor
Bowling Association
H.Q. 3
Scirocco Close
Moulton Park
Northampton
NN3 6AP

Tel: 01604-494163
Fax: 01604-494434

Mrs N Colling
Honorary Secretary
English Womens Bowling
Association
The Royal Pump Rooms
Leamington Spa
Warwickshire
CV32 4AB

Tel: 01926-430686
Home Tel: 01297-21317

Mrs I Younger
Secretary
English Womens Bowling
Federation
Irela
Holburn Crescent
Ryton
Tyne and Wear
NE40 3DH

Tel: 0191-413 3160

Boxing

Mr C Brown
Company Secretary
Amateur Boxing
Association of England Ltd
Crystal Palace National
Sports Centre
London
SE19 2BB

Tel: 0181-778 0251
Fax: 0181-778 9324

Mr J Morris
General Secretary
British Boxing Board of
Control
Jack Petersen House
52A Borough High Street
London
SE1 1XW

Tel: 0171-403 5879
Fax: 0171-378 6670

Camping and Caravanning

Mr C A Smith OBE
Director General
Camping and Caravanning
Club
Greenfields House
Westwood Way
Coventry
CV4 8JH

Tel: 01203-694995
Fax: 01203-694886

Canoeing

Mr P Owen
Chief Executive
British Canoe Union
John Dudderidge House
Adbolton Lane
West Bridgford
Nottingham
NG2 5AS

Tel: 0115-982 1100
Fax: 0115-982 1797

Caving

Mr F S Baguley
Honorary Secretary
National Caving
Association
White Lion House
Ynys Uchaf
Ystradgynlais
Swansea
SA9 1RW

Home Tel: 01639-849519

Chinese Martial Arts

Mr B Weatherall
Secretary
British Council of Chinese
Martial Arts
46 Oaston Road
Nuneaton
Warwickshire
CV11 6JZ

Tel: 01203-329461

Cricket

Mr A Smith
Secretary
Cricket Council, The
Lords Cricket Ground
London
NW8 8QN

Tel: 0171-286 4405

Mr T N Bates
Director of Administration
& Development
National Cricket
Association
Lords Cricket Ground
London
NW8 8QZ

Tel: 0171-289 6098

Mr A Smith
Chief Executive
Test and County Cricket
Board
Lords Cricket Ground
London
NW8 8QN

Tel: 0171-286 4405

Ms B Daniels
Executive Director
Women's Cricket
Association
Warwickshire County
Cricket Ground
Edgbaston Road
Birmingham
B5 7QX

Tel: 0121-440 0567
Fax: 0121-440 0520

Croquet

Mr L W D Antenen
Secretary
Croquet Association, The
Hurlingham Club
Ranelagh Gardens
London
SW6 3PR

Tel: 0171-736 3148
Fax: 0171-736 3148

Curling

Mrs M Kidd
Secretary
British Curling Association
Cairnie House
Avenue K
Ingliston Showground
Newbridge
Midlothian
EH28 2NB
Scotland

Tel: 0131-333 3303
Fax: 0131-333 3323

Mr E G Hinds
Secretary
English Curling Association
Little Wethers
Sandy Lane
Northwood
Middx
HA6 3HA

Fax: 01895-273481
Home Tel: 01923-825004
Work Tel: 01895-256541

Cycling

Mr G Beckett
General Secretary
Bicycle Polo Association of
Great Britain
5 Archer Road
South Norwood
London
SE25 4JN

Home Tel: 0181-656 9724

Mr R Witham
Administrator
British Cycle Speedway
Council
57 Rectory Lane
Poringland
Norwich
NR14 7SW

Tel: 01508-493880
Fax: 01508-493880

Mr J Hendry
Chief Executive
British Cycling Federation
National Cycling Centre
1 Stuart Street
Manchester
M11 4DQ

Tel: 0161-230 2301
Fax: 0161-231 0591

Mr B Furness
General Secretary
British Cyclo-Cross
Association
14 Deneside Road
Darlington
Co Durham
DL3 9HZ

Tel: 01325-482052
Fax: 01325-482052
Home Tel: 01325-465958

Administration Officer
British Mountain Bike
Federation
National Cycling Centre
1 Stuart Street
Manchester
M11 4DQ

Tel: 0161-223 2244
Fax: 0161-231 0592

Mr A Harlow
Director
Cyclists Touring Club
Cotterell House
69 Meadrow
Godalming
Surrey
GU7 3HS

Tel: 01483-417217
Fax: 01483-426994

Mrs V Hyde
National Secretary
English BMX Association
61 Mayfield Gardens
Hanwell
London
W7 3RB

Tel: 0181-813 2838
Fax: 0181-813 2838

Mrs S Knight
General Secretary
English Schools Cycling
Association
21 Bedhampton Road
North End
Portsmouth
Hants
PO2 7JX

Tel: 01705-642226

Mr P A Heaton
National Secretary
Road Time Trials Council
77 Arlington Drive
Pennington
Leigh
Lancs
WN7 3QP

Tel: 01942-603976
Fax: 01942-262326

Dance – see **Movement, Dance** etc

Sport for the Disabled

Ms A Wood
Acting Chief Executive
British Sports Association
for the Disabled
Head Office
Solecast House
13–27 Brunswick Place
London
N1 6DX

Tel: 0171-490 4919
Fax: 0171-490 4914

Mr M Southam
National Officer
United Kingdom Sports
Association for People with
Learning Disability
Solecast House
13–27 Brunswick Place
London
N1 6DX

Tel: 0171-250 1100
Fax: 0171-250 0110

Dragon Boat Racing

Ms S Sheard
Management Executive
British Dragon Boat Racing
Association
5th Floor
125 Pall Mall
London
SW17 5EA

Tel: 0171-930 2296
Fax: 0171-930 4777

Driving (Equestrian) – see
Equestrian

Driving (Motor) – see
Motor Sports

Equestrian

Colonel T J S Eastwood
Chief Executive
British Horse Society
British Equestrian Centre
Stoneleigh
Kenilworth
Warwickshire
CV8 2LR

Tel: 01203-696697

Mr A R Finding
Secretary General
British Show Jumping
Association
British Equestrian Centre
Stoneleigh
Kenilworth
Warwickshire
CV8 2LR

Tel: 01203-696516
Fax: 01203-696685

Mr J R Moss
Director
Riding for the Disabled
Association
National Agricultural
Centre
Avenue R
Stoneleigh Park
Kenilworth
Warwickshire
CV8 2LY

Tel: 01203-696510
Fax: 01203-696532

Eton Fives – see **Fives**

Fencing

Miss G M Kenneally
Secretary
Amateur Fencing
Association
1 Barons Gate
33–35 Rothschild Road
London
W4 5HT

Tel: 0181-742 3032
Fax: 0181-742 3033

Fives

Mr R Beament
Honorary Secretary
Eton Fives Association
74 Clarence Road
St Albans
Herts
AL1 4NG

Tel: 01727-837099
Home Tel: 01727-837099

Mr M Beaman
General Secretary
Rugby Fives Association
The Old Forge
Sutton Valence
Maidstone
Kent
ME17 3AW

Home Tel: 01622-842278

Flying

Mr J Bell
Chief Executive
British Microlight Aircraft
Association
The Bullring
Deddington
Banbury
Oxon
OX15 0TT

Tel: 01869-338888
Fax: 01869-337116

Mr G Lynn MBE
General Secretary
British Model Flying
Association
Chacksfield House
31 St Andrews Road
Leicester
LE2 8RE

Tel: 0116-244 0028
Fax: 0116-244 0645

Mr B Smith
Vice President
Popular Flying Association
Shoreham Airport
Shoreham-by-Sea
W Sussex
BN43 5FF

Tel: 01273-461616
Fax: 01273-463390

Mr B Rolfe
Secretary
Royal Aero Club of the
United Kingdom
Kimberley House
47 Vaughan Way
Leicester
LE1 4SG

Work Tel: 0116-253 1051

Football – see **Association Football**

Gaelic Football

Mr T Daly
Gaelic Athletic Association
Gaelic Football Ground
West End Road
Ruislip
Middx
HA4 6QX

Tel: 0181-841 2468
Fax: 0181-842 2622

Gliding

Mr B Rolfe
Secretary
British Gliding Association
Kimberley House
47 Vaughan Way
Leicester
LE1 4SE

Tel: 0116-253 1051
Fax: 0116-251 5939
Work Tel: 0116-253 1051

Golf

Mr P M Baxter
Secretary
English Golf Union
The National Golf Centre
The Broadway
Woodhall Spa
Lincs
LN1 6PU

Tel: 01526-354500
Fax: 01526-354020

Mrs M J Carr
Secretary
English Ladies Golf
Association
Edgbaston Golf Club
Church Road
Edgbaston
Birmingham
B15 3TB

Tel: 0121-456 2088

Miss L E C Attwood MBE
Executive Director
Golf Foundation, The
Foundation House
Hanbury Manor
Ware
Herts
SG12 0UH

Tel: 01920-484044
Fax: 01920-484055

Mrs E Mackie
Administrator
Ladies Golf Union
The Scores
St Andrews
Fife
KY16 9AT

Tel: 01334-75811
Fax: 01334-72818

Mr S Jones
Executive Director
Professional Golfers
Association
Apollo House
The Belfry
Sutton Coldfield
W Midlands
B76 9PT

Tel: 01675-470333

Mr T Coates
Chief Executive
Women Professional Golfers
European Tour
The Tytherington Club
Dorchester Way
Tytherington
Macclesfield
Cheshire
SK10 2JP

Tel: 01625-611444
Fax: 01625-610406

Gymnastics

Mr D J Minnery AFA
General Secretary
British Amateur Gymnastics
Association
Registered Office
Ford Hall
Lilleshall National Sports
Centre
Newport
Shropshire
TF10 9BNB

Tel: 01952-820330
Fax: 01952-820326

Handball

Mr B J Rowland
Chairman
British Handball
Association
40 Newchurch Road
Rawtenshall
Rossendale
Lancs
BB4 7QX

Tel: 01706-229354
Fax: 01706-229354

Hang/Para Gliding

Ms J Burdett
Secretary
British Hang Gliding and
Paragliding Association
The Old School Room
Loughborough Road
Leicester
LE4 5PJ

Tel: 0116-261 1322
Fax: 0116-261 1323

Hockey

English Hockey
Association, The
The Stadium
Silbury Boulevard
Milton Keynes
Bucks
MK9 1HA

Tel: 01908-241100
Fax: 01908-241106

See also **Ice Hockey and
Roller Hockey**

Horse Racing

Mr T Ricketts
Chief Executive
British Horseracing Board
42 Portman Square
London
W1H 0EN

Tel: 0171-396 0011

Hovering

Mrs B A Kemp
Secretary
Hover Club of Great Britain
Ltd
10 Long Acre
Bingham
Nottingham
NG13 8BG

Home Tel: 01949-837294

Ice Hockey

Mr D Pickles
Secretary
British Ice Hockey
Association
Second Floor Suite
517 Christchurch Road
Boscombe
Bournemouth
BH1 4AG

Tel: 01202-303946
Fax: 01202-398005

Ice Skating

Ms C Godsall
Chief Executive
National Ice Skating
Association of UK Ltd
15–27 Gee Street
London
EC1V 3RE

Tel: 0171-253 3824
Fax: 0171-490 2589

Judo

Ms S Startin
Office Manager
British Judo Association
7A Rutland Street
Leicester
LE1 1RB

Tel: 0116-255 9669
Fax: 0116-255 9660

Ju Jitsu

Mr M Dixon
Chairman
British Ju-Jitsu Association
5 Avenue Parade
Accrington
Lancs
BB5 6PN

Tel: 0114-266 6733
Fax: 0174-266 6733

Kabaddi

National Kabaddi
Association
7 Holling Mill Close
Edgbaston
Birmingham
B5 7QQ

Tel: 0121-446 4642
Fax: 0121-446 4410

Karate

Mr B Porch
General Secretary
English Karate Governing
Body
58 Bloomfield Drive
Bath
Avon
BA2 2BG

Tel: 01225-834008

Kendo

Mr D J Raybould
Secretary
British Kendo Association
Coppice Lodge
Stafford Road
Teddesley
Stafford
ST19 5RP

Tel: 01543-466334

Korfball

Mr G J Crafter
Honorary General Secretary
British Korfball Association
PO Box 179
Maidstone
Kent
ME14 1LU

Work Tel: 01622-813115

Lacrosse

Mrs A Chesses
English Lacrosse
Association
4 Western Court
Bromley Street
Digbeth
Birmingham
B9 4AN

Tel: 0121-773 4422
Fax: 0121-753 0042

Land Yachting – see **Sand
and Land Yachting**

Lawn Tennis

Mr J C U James
Secretary
Lawn Tennis Association
The Queens Club
Barons Court
West Kensington
London
W14 9EG

Tel: 0171-381 7000
Fax: 0171-381 5965

Life Saving

Ms H Bardley
Deputy Directory General
Royal Life Saving Society
UK
Mountbatten House
Studley
Warwickshire
B80 7NN

Tel: 01527-853943
Fax: 01527-854453

Luge

Mr J G Evans
General Secretary
Great Britain Luge
Association
Mortimer House
Holmer Road
Hereford
HR4 9SB

Tel: 01432-353539
Work Tel: 01432-353920

Modern Pentathlon

Ms C Banks
Chair
Modern Pentathlon
Association of Great Britain
Pentathlon House
Baughurst Road
Baughurst
Basingstoke
Hants
RG26 5JF

Tel: 01734-817181

Motor Cycling

Mr D R Barnfield
Chief Executive
Auto-Cycle Union
ACU House
Wood Street
Rugby
Warwickshire
CV21 2YX

Tel: 01788-540519
Fax: 01788-573585

Mr G Reeve
Speedway Control Board
ACU Headquarters
Wood Street
Rugby
Warwickshire
CV21 2YX

Tel: 01788-540096
Fax: 01788-540096

Motor Sports

Mr J R Quenby
Chief Executive
RAC Motor Sports
Association Ltd
Motor Sports House
Riverside Park
Colnbrook
Slough
SL3 0HG

Tel: 01753-681736
Fax: 01753-682938

Mountaineering

Mr R Payne
General Secretary
British Mountaineering
Council
177–179 Burton Road
West Didsbury
Manchester
M20 2BB

Tel: 0161-445 4747
Fax: 0161-445 4500

Movement, Dance, Exercise and Fitness

Ms P Pique
Secretary
Dalcroze Society, The
41A Woodmansterne Road
Coulsdon
Surrey
CR5 2DJ

Tel: 0181-645 0714

Mrs R Thomas
Chair
English Amateur
Dancesport Association
515 Abbeydale Road
Sheffield
S7 1FU

Mr J Ripley
Chief Officer
English Folk Dance and
Song Society
Cecil Sharp House
2 Regent's Park Road
London
NW1 7AY

Tel: 0171-485 2206
Fax: 0171-284 0523

Ms D Lock
Administrator
Exercise Association of
England Ltd
Unit 4
Angel Gate
City Road
London
EC1V 2PT

Tel: 0171-278 0811
Fax: 0171-278 0726

Ms V Augustine
Administration Officer
Health and Beauty Exercise
52 London Street
Chertsey
Surrey
KT16 8AJ

Tel: 01932-564567
Fax: 01932-567566

Ms S Sheath
Media Liaison Officer
Keep Fit Association
Francis House
Francis Street
London SW1P 1DE

Tel: 0171-233 8898
Fax: 0171-630 7936

Ms L De Oliveira
Secretary
Laban Guild
26 Rodney Road
Ongar
Essex
CM5 9HN

Mr J Hastie
Margaret Morris Movement
PO Box 1525
Garelochead
Helensburgh
Dunbartonshire
G84 0AF

Tel: 01436-810215

Mrs P Palmer
National Development
Officer
Medau Society, The
8B Robson House
East Street
Epsom
Surrey
KT17 1HH

Tel: 01372-729056

Netball

Mrs E M Nicholl
Chief Executive
All England Netball
Association
Netball House
9 Paynes Park
Hitchin
Herts
SG5 1EH

Tel: 01462-442344
Fax: 01462-442343

Octopush – see **Sub-Aqua**

Orienteering

Mr N Cameron
Secretary General
British Orienteering
Federation
Riversdale
Dale Road North
Darley Dale
Matlock
Derbyshire
DE4 2HX

Tel: 01629-734042
Fax: 01629-733769

Parachuting

Mr D Oddy
Office Manager
British Parachute
Association
5 Wharf Way
Glen Parva
Leicester
LE2 9TF

Tel: 0116-278 5271
Fax: 0116-247 7662

Paragliding – see **Hang/Para
Gliding**

Petanque

Mr D Kimpton
National Administrator
British Petanque Association
18 Ensign Business Centre
Westwood Park
Coventry
CV4 8JA

Tel: 01203-421408
Fax: 01203-422269

Polo

Mr J W M Crisp
Secretary
Hurlingham Polo
Association
Winterlake
Kirtlington
Kidlington
Oxford
OX5 3HG

Tel: 01869-350044
Fax: 01869-350625

Pool

Mr I Powell
Secretary
English Pool Association
44 Jones House
Penkridge Street
Walsall
WS2 8JX

Work Tel: 01922-35587

Quoits

Mr A Burton
Secretary
National Quoits Association
2 Blackmore Close
Guisborough
Cleveland
TS14 7LR

Work Tel: 01287-633796

Racketball

Mr I Wright
British Racketball
Association
50 Tredegar Road
Wilmington
Dartford
DA2 7AZ

Fax: 01322-289295
Home Tel: 01322-272200

Racquetball

Ms W Hackett
General Secretary
Great Britain Racquetball
Federation
10 Waverley Gardens
Barking
Essex
IG11 0BQ

Tel: 0181-925 9842

Rackets

Brigadier A D Myrtle CB
CBE
Chief Executive
Tennis and Rackets
Association
c/o The Queens Club
Palliser Road
West Kensington
London
W14 9EQ

Tel: 0171-386 3448

Rambling

Mr L Maple
Honorary Secretary
Long Distance Walkers
Association
21 Upcroft
Windsor
Berks
SL4 3NH

Home Tel: 01753-866685

Mr A Mattingly
Director
Ramblers' Association, The
1–5 Wandsworth Road
London
SW8 2XX

Tel: 0171-582 6878
Fax: 0171-587 3799

Real Tennis

Brigadier A D Myrtle CB
CBE
Chief Executive
Tennis and Rackets
Association
c/o The Queens Club
Palliser Road
West Kensington
London
W14 9EQ

Tel: 0171-386 3448

Riding and Driving – see Equestrian

Roller Hockey

Dr R Wheatley CChem
MRSC
President
National Roller Hockey
Association
528 Loose Road
Maidstone
Kent
ME15 9UF

Home Tel: 01622-743155

Roller Skating

Ms M Brooks
Chairman
British Federation of Roller
Skating
Lilleshall National Sports
Centre
Newport
Shropshire
TF10 9AT

Tel: 01952-825253
Fax: 01952-825228

Rounders

Mr B MacKinney
National Development
Officer
National Rounders
Association
3 Denehurst Avenue
Nottingham
NG8 5DA

Tel: 0115-978 5514
Work Tel: 0115-978 5514

Rowing

Mrs R E Napp
Senior Administrative
Officer
Amateur Rowing
Association
The Priory
6 Lower Mall
Hammersmith
London
W6 9DJ

Tel: 0181-748 3632
Fax: 0181-741 4658

Rugby Fives – see Fives

Rugby League

Mr M F Oldroyd
Chief Executive
British Amateur Rugby
League Association
West Yorkshire House
4 New North Parade
Huddersfield
HD1 5JP

Tel: 01484-544131

Mr M Lindsay
Chief Executive
Rugby Football League, The
Red Hall
Red Hall Lane
Leeds
LS17 8NB

Tel: 0113-232 9111
Fax: 0113-232 3666

Rugby Union

Mr T Hallett
Secretary
Rugby Football Union, The
Rugby Road
Twickenham
Middx
TW1 1DZ

Tel: 0181-892 8161
Fax: 0181-892 9816

Sailing/Yachting

Brigadier R Duchesne OBE
Secretary General
Royal Yachting Association
RYA House
Romsey Road
Eastleigh
Hants
SO50 9YA

Tel: 01703-629962
Fax: 01703-629924

Mr A Hillman
Manager
RYA Windsurfing
RYA House
Romsey Road
Eastleigh
Hants
SO50 9YA

Tel: 01703-629962
Fax: 01703-629924

Sand and Land Yachting

Mr M Hampton
Secretary
British Federation of Sand
and Land Yacht Clubs
23 Piper Drive
Long Whatton
Loughborough
Leics
LE12 5DJ

Tel: 01509-842292

Shooting

Mr J A Swift
Director
British Association for
Shooting and Conservation
Marford Mill
Rossett
Wrexham
Clwyd
LL12 0HL

Tel 01244-570881

Mr E Orduna
Executive Technical Officer
Clay Pigeon Shooting
Association
Unit O
Earlstrees Court
Earlstrees Road Industrial
Estate
Corby
Northants
NN17 4AX

Tel: 01536-443566
Fax: 01536-443438

Mr R Hanley
Honorary Secretary
English Shooting Council
c/o London and Middlesex
RA
Bisley Camp
Brookwood
Woking
Surrey
GU24 0PA

Tel: 01483-473006
Fax: 01483-472427

Mr K Murray
Honorary Secretary
Great Britain Target
Shooting Federation
1 The Cedars
Great Wakering
Southend-on-Sea
SS3 0AQ

Home Tel: 01702-219395

Mr C C C Cheshire OBE
Chief Executive
National Rifle Association
Bisley Camp
Brookwood
Woking
Surrey
GU24 0PB

Tel: 01483-797777
Fax: 01483-797285

Mr J Hoare
Secretary
National Small-Bore Rifle
Association
Lord Roberts House
Bisley Camp
Brookwood
Woking
Surrey
GU24 0NP

Tel: 01483-476969
Fax: 01483-476392

Skating – see Ice Skating and Roller Skating

Ski Bob

Miss G Rawson
Secretary
Ski Bob Association of
Great Britain
40 Durkar Low Lane
Durkar
Wakefield
W Yorkshire
WF4 3BL

Ski-ing

Mr M Jardine
Chief Executive
British Ski Federation
258 Main Street
East Calder
Livingston
West Lothian
EH53 0EE

Tel: 01506-884343
Fax: 01506-882952

Mrs D King
Chief Executive
English Ski Council
Area Library Building
Queensway Mall
The Cornbow
Halesowen
W Midlands
B63 4AJ

Tel: 0121-501 2314
Fax: 0121-585 6448

Snooker – see **Billiards and Snooker**

Soccer – see **Association Football**

Softball

Ms N Harper
President
British Softball Federation
PO Box 10064
London
N6 5JN

Tel: 0181-341 7931
Fax: 0181-348 4522

Sombo Wrestling

Mr M Clarke
Chairman
British Sombo Federation
Clarkes Sports Studio
Vicarage Road
Milton Regis
Sittingbourne
Kent
ME10 2BL

Tel: 01795-470659
Fax: 01795-421644

Squash

Mr N Moore
General Secretary
Squash Rackets Association
PO Box 1106
London
W3 0ZD

Tel: 0181-746 1616
Fax: 0181-746 0580

Stoolball

Mrs D Saunders
Chairman
National Stoolball Association
3 Bramber Way
Burgess Hill
W Sussex
RH15 8JU

Street Hockey

Mrs S van der Geyten
General Secretary
British Skater Hockey Association
Grammont
Chiddingley Road
Horam
Heathfield
E Sussex
TN21 0JH

Tel: 01435-812945
Fax: 01435-812359

Sub-aqua

Mr H Painter
Chairman
British Sub-Aqua Club
Telfords Quay
Ellesmere Port
South Wirral
L65 4FY

Tel: 0151-357 1951
Fax: 0151-357 1250

Surfing

Mr C K Wilson
Administrator
British Surfing Association
Champions Yard
Penzance
Cornwall
TR18 2TA

Tel: 01736-60250
Fax: 01736-331077

Surf Life Saving

Mrs E D Little
National Secretary
Surf Life Saving Association
of Great Britain Ltd
Verney House
115 Sidwell Street
Exeter
EX4 6RY

Tel: 01392-54364
Fax: 01392-496563

Swimming

Mr D Sparkes
Director of Operations
Amateur Swimming
Association
Harold Fern House
Derby Square
Loughborough
Leics
LE11 0AL

Tel: 01509-230431
Fax: 01509-610720

Table Tennis

Mr R Sinclair
General Secretary
English Table Tennis
Association
Third Floor
Queensbury House
Havelock Road
Hastings
E Sussex
TN34 1HF

Tel: 01424-722525
Fax: 01424-422103

Taekwondo

Mr M Dew
British Taekwondo Council
163A Church Road
Redfield
Bristol
Avon
BS9 5DU

Tel: 0117-955 1046
Fax: 0117-955 0589

Tang Soo Do

Mr P V M Chin
Secretary General
United Kingdom Tang Soo
Do Federation
PO Box 184
Watford
WD1 3LS

Home Tel: 01582-402248

Tchouk-ball

Mr G B Osbourne
Secretary
British Tchouk-Ball
Association
65 Shaw Green Lane
Prestbury
Cheltenham
Glos
GL52 2BS

Tel: 01242-231154

Tennis – see Lawn Tennis

**Tennis and Rackets – see
Real Tennis, Rackets**

Tenpin Bowling

General Secretary
British Tenpin Bowling
Association
114 Balfour Road
Ilford
Essex
IG1 4JD

Tel: 0181-478 1745
Fax: 0181-514 3665

Tobogganing – see Luge

Trampolining

Mr R C Walker
Secretary
British Trampoline
Federation Ltd
146 College Road
Harrow
Middx
HA1 1BH

Tel: 0181-863 7278

Triathlon

Ms E Shaw
Chief Executive
British Triathlon
Association Ltd
PO Box 26
Ashby-de-la-Zouch
Leics
LE65 2ZR

Tel: 01530-414234
Fax: 01530-560279

Tug-of-War

Mr P J Craft
Secretary
Tug-of-War Association
57 Lynton Road
Chesham
Bucks
HP5 2BT

Work Tel: 01494-783057

**Underwater Swimming –
see Sub-Aqua**

Unihoc

Mr L Bennet
Secretary
English Unihoc Association
15 Grovely Cottages
Great Wishford
Salisbury
SP2 0NT

Volleyball

Mr G Bulman
Director
English Volleyball
Association
27 South Road
West Bridgford
Nottingham
NG2 7AG

Tel: 0115-981 6324
Fax: 0115-945 5429

Water Skiing

Ms G Hill
Executive Officer
British Water Ski Federation
390 City Road
London
EC1V 2QA

Tel: 0171-833 2855
Fax: 0171-837 5879

Weightlifting

Mrs J Gaul
British Amateur Weight
Lifters Association
Grosvenor House
131 Hurst Street
Oxford
OX4 1HE

Tel: 01865-200339
Fax: 01865-790096

Windsurfing – see
Sailing/Yachting

Wrestling

Mr R Tomlinson
Development and Public
Relations Officer
British Amateur Wrestling
Association
41 Great Clowes Street
Salford
M7 9RQ

Tel: 0161-832 9209
Fax: 0161-833 1120

Mrs C Barfoot
Secretary
English Olympic Wrestling
Association
41 Great Clowes Street
Salford
M7 9RQ

Tel: 0161-832 9209
Fax: 0161-833 1120

Yachting – see
Sailing/Yachting

Yoga

Liaison Officer
British Wheel of Yoga
1 Hamilton Place
Boston Road
Sleaford
Lincs
NG34 7ES

Tel: 01529-306851

INDEX